1488
This edition published in 1992 by Tiger Books International PLC, London
© 1986 Coombe Books
Printed in Singapore
All rights reserved
ISBN 1-85501-215-4

TEXT BY
Carolyn Garner

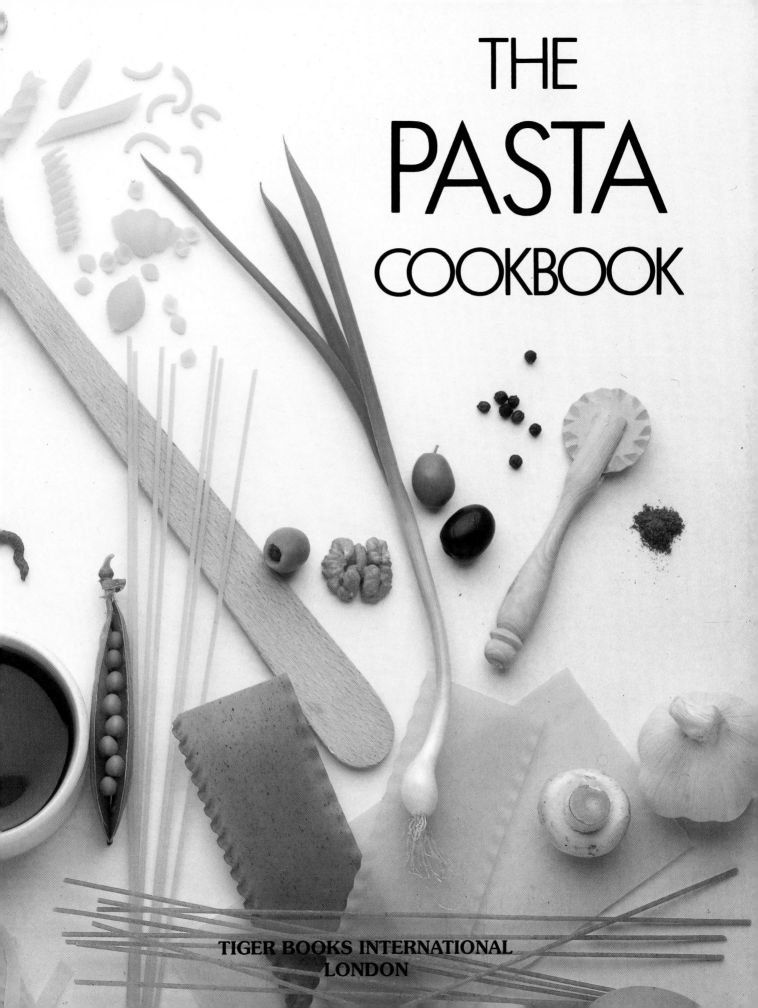

THE
PASTA
COOKBOOK

TIGER BOOKS INTERNATIONAL
LONDON

Contents

Introduction

Pasta: one of the world's most basic yet versatile foods.

With the increased migration of people and ideas, and a greater interest in foods of other nations, it is no surprise that pasta cookery has become so fashionable.

The increased demand, having resulted in the availability of necessary ingredients, means that the enthusiastic cook can launch into myriad culinary adventures with 'pasta' – the chameleon of the cookery world.

Although chiefly an Italian product, pasta has become an ubiquitous term, with the cuisines of many other countries often including noodles.

Pasta is literally a paste made with flour and eggs. Commercial pasta is made from a hard wheat called durum wheat, but fresh pasta may be made with any kind of flour. It is sometimes made in different colours, green (pasta verde) with the addition of spinach; and pink (pasta rosa) which has tomato paste added, to name just a couple. Pasta is now readily available dried and fresh, or can be made in the home with some practice.

It takes little time to cook and should on no account be overcooked as there is nothing worse than a congealed mass of pasta. Always use a large, uncovered saucepan, lots of boiling salted water and a few drops of oil to separate the pasta and prevent the water boiling over. The water should not be boiling too rapidly and a careful stir will also help prevent the pasta from sticking together. The pasta will be ready when tender but still firm, or 'al dente' – firm to the bite.

Pour immediately into a colander to prevent further cooking, and rinse under hot water to remove any excess starch. It should then be served immediately. However, if it needs to be kept, put it in a bowl of hand-hot water until needed.

The longer pastas, such as spaghetti, should be held at one end and put into rapidly boiling water, gently coiled around the pan as it softens, then simmered until 'al dente'. It should not be broken up.

Fresh pasta cooks a lot quicker than dried pasta. Wholemeal pasta takes longer, and the cooking time will vary a lot according to the thickness of the pasta type.

The amount of pasta per person will vary according to circumstances – individual appetites and what the pasta is being served with must play a leading part in how much should be cooked.

There are a great many pasta shapes, and their Italian names often differ from one region to another. It may, therefore, be prudent to search for the shape of the less known varieties of pasta rather than to try to memorise the names.

The most common ingredients used are tomatoes (generally Italian plum tomatoes), onions, mushrooms and Parmesan cheese. However, I would like to mention a few important ingredients. Of the cheeses, Parmesan (Parmigiano), pecorino and ricotta are most frequently used. Parmesan cheese is made from cow's milk and is used for grating and cooking, as it melts well without becoming stringy. Pecorino, a sheep's milk cheese, is also used for grating and, with a sharper flavour than Parmesan cheese, heightens the spicy dishes. Ricotta, a fresh unripened cheese, is made from the whey of cow's milk. As it is smooth and has a mild taste it is used in a number of savoury and sweet dishes.

Of course, one fundamental ingredient that must be mentioned here is olive oil. The distinct flavour of the green olive has enhanced many a pasta dish. Good olive oil is a greeny-yellow in colour, the best variety being the first pressing or virgin olive oil.

**Tortellini with Mushroom Sauce (right) and
Ravioli with Ricotta Cheese (top right).**

Soups and Elegant Starters

Chick-Pea Soup

PREPARATION TIME: Chick-peas soaked overnight plus 5 minutes

COOKING TIME: 1 hour 20 minutes

140g (5oz) dried chick-peas
115g (4oz) soup pasta
2 cloves garlic
45ml (3 tbsps) olive oil
1 tsp basil
400g (12oz) can plum tomatoes, chopped
1 litre (1½ pints) water
1 chicken stock cube
2 tbsps Parmesan cheese, grated
Salt and pepper

Soak chick-peas overnight in enough water to cover by 25mm (1 inch). Discard water in which the chick-peas have soaked. Place the chick-peas in a large, heavy pan, and cover with 25mm (1 inch) of water. Bring to the boil and simmer, covered, for about 1 hour until chick-peas are tender, ensuring that they do not boil dry. Heat olive oil in a heavy pan, and sauté garlic cloves. When browned, remove and discard garlic cloves. Add tomatoes and their juice, water and basil, and cook together for 20 minutes. Add drained chick-peas, crumbled stock cube, and salt and pepper to taste. Stir well; simmer a further 10 minutes. Bring back to boil. Add pasta, and cook, stirring frequently, for 10 minutes. Mix in half of the Parmesan cheese. Adjust seasoning, and serve immediately, with remaining Parmesan cheese sprinkled on top. Serves 4.
Note: Soup may be puréed before pasta is added, if desired.

Tagliatelle with Egg and Caviar

PREPARATION TIME: 5 minutes

COOKING TIME: 15 minutes

225g (8oz) red tagliatelle
30g (1oz) red caviar or lumpfish roe
4 small eggs, hard boiled
60g (2oz) butter or margarine
Black pepper

Put eggs into boiling water and cook for 12 minutes. Rinse under

cold water, to stop further cooking. Remove shells, cut in half, and scoop out yolks with a teaspoon. Push yolks through a sieve. Wash egg-whites, and cut into strips. Set aside. Cook tagliatelle in plenty of boiling salted water until *al dente*. Rinse in hot water, and drain well. Heat butter in pan, add freshly-ground black pepper and tagliatelle. Add egg whites, and toss well. Sprinkle caviar over, and top with egg-yolk. Serve immediately. Serves 4 as a starter.

Minestra

PREPARATION TIME: 15 minutes

COOKING TIME: 45 minutes

115g (4oz) short-cut/elbow macaroni
30ml (2 tbsps) olive oil
1 onion
1 carrot
1 stick celery
1½ litres (3 pints) water
225g (8oz) fresh spinach
2 tomatoes
1 tsp rosemary
2 tbsps chopped parsley
2 cloves garlic, crushed
60g (2oz) Parmesan cheese, grated
Salt and pepper

Cut onion, carrot and celery into thick matchstick strips. Heat oil in a large, heavy pan, and fry vegetable strips until just browning, stirring occasionally. Pour on water, add salt and pepper, and let simmer for 20 minutes. Meanwhile, wash and cut spinach leaves into shreds, add to soup and cook for 10 minutes. Scald and skin tomatoes, and chop roughly, removing seeds. Add tomatoes, macaroni, garlic, parsley and rosemary to the soup, and simmer a further 10 minutes. Adjust seasoning. Serve with grated Parmesan cheese if desired.

Meatball Soup

PREPARATION TIME: 10 minutes

COOKING TIME: 1 hour 40 minutes

OVEN: 180°C, 350°F, Gas Mark 3

225g (8oz) minced beef
60g (2oz) breadcrumbs
1 egg, beaten
450g (1lb) beef bones
1 stick celery
1 carrot
1 onion
15ml (1 tbsp) oil
400g (14oz) can plum tomatoes
175g (6oz) soup pasta
1 tbsp chopped parsley
Salt and pepper

Place bones, peeled carrot, onion and celery in a large saucepan and cover with cold water. Bring to the boil: cover and simmer for one hour at least. Meanwhile, mix together lightly beaten egg with minced beef, breadcrumbs and plenty of seasoning. Roll a teaspoon amount into small balls and place on a roasting tin with the oil. Bake in a preheated oven for 45 minutes, turning occasionally. Strain stock into a saucepan. Push tomatoes and their juice through sieve, and add to stock. Bring to the boil, and simmer for 15 minutes. Add pasta and cook for 10 minutes, stirring frequently. Add meatballs, adjust seasoning, and stir in chopped parsley. Serve hot.

This page: Tagliatelle with Egg and Caviar.

Facing page: Minestra (top), Meatball Soup (centre right) and Chick-Pea Soup (bottom).

Tomato Soup

PREPARATION TIME: 15 minutes
COOKING TIME: 45 minutes

115g (4oz) short-cut/elbow macaroni
30g (1oz) butter or margarine
1 small onion, peeled and chopped
1 small green pepper, cored, seeds
    removed, and chopped
15g (½oz) flour
1 litre (2 pints) brown stock, or water
    plus 2 beef stock cubes
450g (1lb) tomatoes, chopped
2 tbsps tomato purée
1 tbsp grated horseradish
Salt and pepper

Garnish:

2 tbsps soured cream,
1 tbsp chopped parsley

Heat the butter in a pan. Cover and
cook the onion and green pepper
for 5 minutes. Add the flour and
stir. Add stock, tomatoes and
tomato purée. Simmer for 15
minutes. Purée soup and pass
through a sieve. Return to pan, and
season with salt and pepper to
taste. Add macaroni 10 minutes
before serving. Simmer and stir
occasionally. Add horseradish
before serving. Garnish with soured
cream and parsley. Serve
immediately.

Tagliatelle with Smoked Salmon and Caviar

PREPARATION TIME: 5 minutes
COOKING TIME: 15 minutes

225g (8oz) green tagliatelle
90g (3oz) smoked salmon, cut into
    strips
Juice of half a lemon
30g (1oz) red caviar or lumpfish roe
30g (1oz) butter or margarine
2 tbsps double cream
Black pepper

Garnish:

Lemon slices

Cook tagliatelle in lots of boiling
salted water for 10 minutes, or until
tender but still firm. Rinse under
hot water, and drain well. Heat
butter in pan, and add lemon juice
and freshly-ground black pepper.
Return tagliatelle to pan, and add
smoked salmon. Toss together.
Serve topped with double cream
and a sprinkling of red caviar.
Garnish with lemon slices. Serve
immediately. Serves 4 as a starter.

Shell Pasta with Taramasalata

PREPARATION TIME: 15 minutes
COOKING TIME: 15 minutes

225g (8oz) shell pasta
225g (8oz) taramasalata
30ml (2 tbsps) lemon juice
10 black olives, pips removed, and
    chopped
1 tbsp black caviar or lumpfish roe

To Make Taramasalata:

225g (8oz) smoked cod roe
Half onion, grated
225g (8oz) white bread, crusts
    removed
60ml (4 tbsps) milk
90ml (6 tbsps) olive oil
30ml (2 tsps) lemon juice
Black pepper

Crumble bread into a bowl and
add milk. Set aside to soak. Scoop
the cod roe out of its skin, and
break it down with a wooden
spoon. Squeeze the bread dry in a
sieve. Add onion and bread to cod
roe, and mix well. Add oil and
lemon juice very gradually,
alternating between the two. Beat
until smooth and creamy. Add
pepper to taste, and salt if
necessary. Cook pasta shells in lots
of boiling salted water for 10
minutes or until al dente. Rinse in
hot water, and drain well. Sprinkle
over lemon juice; toss together
with taramasalata, and garnish with
caviar and black olives. Serve
immediately. Serves 4 as a starter.

Bean Soup

PREPARATION TIME: 15 minutes
COOKING TIME: 1 hour 45 minutes

430g (15oz) can kidney beans
60g (2oz) bacon, rind removed, and
    chopped
1 stick celery, chopped
1 small onion, peeled and chopped
1 clove garlic, crushed
90g (3oz) can plum tomatoes,
    chopped and seeds removed
1 litre (2 pints) water
1 chicken stock cube
1 tbsp chopped parsley
1 tsp basil
115g (4oz) wholemeal ring pasta
Salt and pepper

Place kidney beans, bacon, celery,
onion, garlic, parsley, basil,
tomatoes and water in a large pan.
Bring to the boil and add stock
cube and salt and pepper to taste.
Cover and cook over a low heat for
about 1½ hours. Raise heat and add
pasta, stirring well. Stir frequently
until pasta is cooked but still
firm – about 10 minutes. Serve
immediately.

**Tagliatelle with Smoked Salmon and
Caviar (top left), Shell Pasta with
Taramasalata (left). Top picture: Bean Soup
(top) and Tomato Soup (bottom).**

Seafood

Spaghetti Marinara

PREPARATION TIME: 10 minutes

COOKING TIME: 20 minutes

300g (10oz) spaghetti
450g (1lb) prawns, shelled and
  de-veined
225g (8oz) scallops, cleaned and
  sliced
45g (1½oz) can anchovy fillets
400g (14oz) can plum tomatoes,
  seeded and chopped
75ml (5 tbsps) dry white wine
75ml (5 tbsps) water
1 bay leaf
4 peppercorns
30ml (2 tbsps) olive oil
1 tsp basil
2 cloves garlic, crushed
1 tbsp tomato purée
1 tbsp chopped parsley
Salt and pepper

Drain anchovies and cut into small pieces. Place water, wine, bay leaf and peppercorns in a pan. Heat to a slow boil. Add scallops and cook for 2 minutes. Remove and drain. Heat the oil, add garlic and basil, and cook for 30 seconds. Add tomatoes, anchovies and tomato purée. Stir until combined. Cook for 10 minutes. Meanwhile, cook the spaghetti in a large pan of boiling salted water for 10 minutes, or until tender but still firm. Drain. Add seafood to sauce, and cook a further 1 minute. Add parsley and stir through. Season with salt and pepper to taste. Toss gently. Pour sauce over spaghetti and serve immediately, sprinkled with parsley.

Pasta Shells with Seafood

PREPARATION TIME: 5 minutes

COOKING TIME: 15 minutes

300g (10oz) pasta shells
450g (1lb) prawns, shelled and
  de-veined
115g (4oz) scallops, cleaned and
  sliced
60g (2oz) butter or margarine
2 cloves garlic, crushed
75ml (5 tbsps) dry white wine

300ml (½ pint) single cream
30ml (2 tbsps) water
1 tbsp cornflour
1 tbsp lemon juice
1 tbsp chopped parsley
Salt and pepper

Melt butter in a pan. Add garlic, and cook for 1 minute. Add wine and cream, and bring back to boil, and cook 2 minutes. Slake cornflour with the water, and pour into sauce. Stir until boiling. Add lemon juice and salt and pepper to taste. Meanwhile, cook the pasta in plenty of boiling salted water, until tender – about 10 minutes. Drain, shaking to remove excess water. Add prawns and scallops to sauce and cook 3 minutes. Pour over pasta shells, toss, and garnish with parsley.

Vermicelli Pescatore

PREPARATION TIME: 15 minutes

COOKING TIME: 40 minutes

115g (4oz) mussels
115g (4oz) cockles
225g (8oz) cod fish fillets
115g (4oz) squid, cleaned
4 large prawns
4 fresh oysters
300g (10oz) vermicelli
250ml (8 fl oz) dry white wine
60ml (4 tbsps) olive oil
2 400g (14oz) cans plum tomatoes
Half a green pepper, diced

Prepare seafood. If using fresh mussels, clean closed mussels, removing beard, and cook in boiling water for 3 minutes until they open. (Discard any that remain closed). Cool and remove from shells, keeping a few in shells for garnish if desired. Skin and bone fillets, and cut fish into 1.5cm (½ inch) pieces. Clean squid and cut into rings. Force tomatoes and their juice through a sieve, and set aside. Heat 30ml (2 tbsps) oil in a pan, and add the squid. Fry gently until golden brown, then add wine, tomato purée, green pepper, and salt and pepper to taste. Simmer for 20 minutes then add fish. Simmer for a further 10 minutes, stirring occasionally. Add cockles and mussels and, when mixture reboils, adjust seasoning. Meanwhile, cook spaghetti in lots of boiling salted water for 10 minutes, or until tender but still firm. Drain well. Add seafood, and toss. Garnish with prawns and fresh oysters.

Sauces and Hearty Meals

Facing page: Farfalle with Beef, Mushroom and Soured Cream (top), Tagliatelle Carbonara (centre left) and Pasta Spirals with Spinach and Bacon (bottom).

Tortiglioni alla Puttanesca

PREPARATION TIME: 10 minutes
COOKING TIME: 15 minutes
SERVES: 4 people

300g (10oz) tortiglioni, spiral pasta
200g (7oz) can plum tomatoes, drained
45g (1½oz) can anchovy fillets, drained
30ml (2 tbsps) olive oil
2 cloves garlic, crushed
½ tsp basil
Pinch chilli powder
115g (4oz) black olives, stoned and chopped
2 tbsps chopped parsley
Salt
Pepper

Chop tomatoes and remove seeds, and chop anchovies. Cook pasta in plenty of boiling salted water for 10 minutes, or until tender but still firm. Rinse in hot water, and drain. Pour into a warmed bowl. Meanwhile, heat oil in pan, add garlic, chilli powder and basil, and cook for 1 minute. Add tomatoes, parsley, olives and anchovies, and cook for a few minutes. Season with salt and pepper. Pour sauce over pasta, and mix together thoroughly. Serve immediately.

Pasta Spirals with Spinach and Bacon

PREPARATION TIME: 15 minutes
COOKING TIME: 15 minutes

300g (10oz) pasta spirals
225g (8oz) spinach
90g (3oz) bacon
1 clove garlic, crushed
1 small red chilli
½ small red pepper
1 small onion
45ml (3 tbsps) olive oil
Salt and pepper

Wash spinach, remove stalks and cut into thin shreds. Core and seed pepper, and slice half finely. Peel onion and chop finely. Remove rind from bacon and chop: Remove seeds from chilli, and slice thinly. Cook pasta spirals in plenty of boiling salted water for 10 minutes, or until tender but still firm. Drain. Meanwhile, heat oil in pan, and add garlic, onion, bacon, chilli and red pepper. Fry for 2 minutes, add spinach, and fry for a further 2 minutes, stirring continuously. Season with salt and pepper to taste. Toss with pasta spirals. Serve immediately.

Tagliatelle Carbonara

PREPARATION TIME: 10 minutes
COOKING TIME: 15 minutes

300g (10oz) tagliatelle
30g (1oz) butter or margarine
115g (4oz) streaky bacon rashers, rind removed, and shredded
15ml (1 tbsp) olive oil
60ml (4 tbsps) single cream
Pinch of paprika
60g (2oz) Parmesan cheese, grated
2 eggs
Salt and pepper

This page: Tortiglioni alla Puttanesca.

Heat oil in a frying-pan, and cook bacon over a moderate heat until browning. Add paprika and cook for 1 minute. Add cream, and stir. Beat together eggs and grated cheese. Meanwhile, cook tagliatelle in lots of boiling salted water for 10 minutes, or until tender but still firm. Drain, return to pan with butter and black pepper, and toss. Add bacon mixture and egg mixture, and toss together. Add salt to taste. Serve immediately.

Farfalle with Beef, Mushroom and Soured Cream

PREPARATION TIME: 10 minutes

COOKING TIME: 15 minutes

300g (10oz) farfalle (pasta butterflies – bows)
225g (8oz) fillet or rump steak, sliced
115g (4oz) mushrooms, sliced
50ml (2 fl oz) soured cream
10 green olives, stoned and chopped
1 onion, peeled and sliced
30g (1oz) unsalted butter
15g (½oz) flour
Salt and pepper

Garnish:
Soured cream
1 tbsp chopped parsley

With a very sharp knife, cut meat into narrow, short strips. Heat half the butter, and fry meat over a high heat until well browned. Set aside. Heat remaining butter in pan, and gently fry onion until soft and just beginning to colour. Add mushrooms, and cook for 3 minutes. Stir in flour and continue frying for a further 3 minutes. Gradually stir in soured cream. When fully incorporated, add meat, olives, and salt and pepper to taste. Meanwhile, cook farfalle in plenty of boiling salted water for 10 minutes, or until tender but still firm. Drain well. Serve with beef and mushroom sauce on top. Garnish with a little extra soured cream and chopped parsley.

Penne with Anchovy Sauce

PREPARATION TIME: 5 minutes

COOKING TIME: 20 minutes

300g (10oz) penne
60g (2oz) can anchovy fillets
400g (14oz) can plum tomatoes
30ml (2 tbsps) olive oil
3 tbsps chopped parsley
60g (2oz) Parmesan cheese, grated
30g (1oz) butter or margarine
Pepper

Chop anchovies and cook them in the oil, stirring to a paste. Sieve tomatoes and add to anchovies, with parsley and freshly-ground black pepper to taste. Bring to the boil and simmer, uncovered, for 10 minutes. Meanwhile, cook the penne in lots of boiling salted water for 10 minutes, or until tender but still firm. Rinse in hot water and drain well. Toss in butter. Combine sauce with the pasta, and sprinkle with parsley, and serve with Parmesan cheese. Serve immediately.

Wholemeal Spaghetti with Peas and Bacon

PREPARATION TIME: 10 minutes

COOKING TIME: 15 minutes

300g (10oz) wholemeal spaghetti
350g (12oz) peas
1 tsp sugar
115g (4oz) bacon, rind removed, and diced
90g (3oz) butter or margarine
Salt and pepper

Garnish:
Parsley

Cook spaghetti in lots of boiling salted water for 10 minutes, or until tender but still firm. Drain. Meanwhile, cook peas in boiling water with a pinch of salt and a teaspoon of sugar. Melt butter in a pan, and fry bacon. When crisp, add peas, and salt and pepper to taste, and pour over spaghetti. Toss through, and serve immediately garnished with chopped parsley if desired.

Penne with Anchovy Sauce (left) and
Wholemeal Spaghetti with Peas and Bacon
(below).

Spaghetti Neapolitana

PREPARATION TIME: 5 minutes

COOKING TIME: 30 minutes

SERVES: 4 people

300g (10oz) spaghetti
2 400g (14oz) cans plum tomatoes
30ml (2 tbsps) olive oil
½ tsp oregano or marjoram
Salt
Pepper
2 tbsps chopped parsley
Parmesan cheese, grated

Push undrained tomatoes through a sieve. Heat oil in pan. Add oregano or marjoram, and cook for 30 seconds. Add puréed tomatoes, and salt and pepper. Bring to boil; reduce heat; simmer uncovered for 20-30 minutes. Meanwhile, cook spaghetti in lots of boiling salted water for about 10 minutes, or until tender but still firm. Rinse under hot water, and drain well. Pour tomato sauce over spaghetti, and toss gently. Sprinkle parsley over the top. Serve with Parmesan cheese. Serve immediately.

Spaghetti with Tomato, Salami and Green Olives

PREPARATION TIME: 15 minutes

COOKING TIME: 15 minutes

300g (10oz) spaghetti
400g (14oz) can plum tomatoes
150g (5oz) salami, sliced and shredded
200g (7oz) green olives, stoned and chopped

1 clove garlic, crushed
30ml (2 tbsps) olive oil
½ tbsp oregano
60g (2oz) pecorino cheese, grated
Salt and pepper

This page: Spaghetti with Tomato, Salami and Green Olives.

Facing page: Spaghetti Neapolitana (top) and Farfalle with Creamy Cheese Sauce (bottom).

Purée tomatoes, and push through a sieve into a saucepan. Add oregano, salami and olives, and heat gently. Add salt and pepper to taste. Meanwhile, cook spaghetti in plenty of boiling salted water for 10 minutes, or until tender but still firm. Drain well. Heat olive oil and freshly-ground black pepper in the pan used to cook the spaghetti. Add spaghetti, and pour the sauce over. Toss well. Serve immediately with pecorino cheese.

Farfalle with Creamy Cheese Sauce

PREPARATION TIME: 5 minutes

COOKING TIME: 15 minutes

SERVES: 4 people

300g (10oz) farfalle (pasta butterflies /bows)
15g (½ oz) butter or margarine
15g (½ oz) flour
300ml (½ pint) milk
60g (2oz) Gruyère or Cheddar cheese, grated
½ tsp French mustard
1 tbsp grated Parmesan cheese

Heat butter in pan. Stir in flour and cook for 1 minute. Remove from heat and gradually stir in milk. Return to heat and stir continuously. Boil for 3 minutes. Stir in Gruyère or Cheddar cheese, and mustard; do not reboil. Meanwhile, cook the pasta in lots of boiling salted water for 10 minutes, or until tender but still firm. Rinse in hot water and drain well. Pour over cheese sauce, and toss. Top with a sprinkling of Parmesan cheese. Serve immediately.

Pasta with Tomato and Yogurt Sauce

PREPARATION TIME: 5 minutes

COOKING TIME: 40 minutes

300g (10oz) pasta shells
45ml (3 tbsps) plain yogurt
15g (½oz) butter or margarine
15g (½oz) flour
150ml (¼ pint) beef stock
400g (14oz) can plum tomatoes
1 bay leaf
Sprig of thyme
Parsley stalks
Salt and pepper

Melt butter in a pan. Stir in the flour, and pour in the stock gradually. Add undrained tomatoes, bay leaf, thyme and parsley stalks. Season with salt and pepper. Bring to the boil, and simmer for 30 minutes. Strain and push through a sieve, adjust seasoning, and re-heat. Meanwhile, cook pasta in plenty of boiling salted water for 10 minutes, or until tender but still firm. Rinse in hot water and drain well. Place in warmed serving dish; pour over tomato sauce, then yogurt. (Yogurt may be marbled through tomato sauce). Serve immediately.

Penne with Chilli Sauce

PREPARATION TIME: 40 minutes

COOKING TIME: 20 minutes

300g (10oz) penne
1 clove garlic, crushed
1 onion, peeled and chopped
450g (1lb) ripe tomatoes
1 aubergine
1 red chilli
30ml (2 tbsps) oil
60g (2oz) pecorino cheese, grated

Trim and cut aubergine into 1.5cm (½ inch) slices, and salt lightly. Leave for 30 minutes. Rinse and wipe dry with absorbent paper. Meanwhile, heat oil in a frying-pan over a moderate heat, and fry garlic and onion until lightly coloured. Peel and seed tomatoes, and chop roughly. Seed chilli, and chop finely. Cut aubergine roughly and add to onion. Fry together for 5 minutes. Add tomatoes and chilli, and mix well. Simmer sauce gently, uncovered, for 5 minutes, stirring occasionally. Meanwhile, cook pasta in lots of boiling salted water for 10 minutes, or until tender but still firm, stirring occasionally. Rinse in hot water, and drain well. Place in a warmed serving dish. Add hot sauce and toss well. Serve immediately with side dish of grated pecorino cheese.

Penne with Chilli Sauce (above) and Pasta with Tomato and Yogurt Sauce (left).

browned all over. Add the tomato purée, salt and pepper to taste, and the stock, and simmer gently for about ¾ hour, until the mixture thickens, stirring occasionally. Add 2 tablespoons sherry, and cook for a further 5 minutes. Meanwhile, place the spaghetti in lots of boiling salted water, and cook for 10 minutes, or until tender but still firm. Drain. Serve with Bolognese sauce on top, and sprinkle with Parmesan cheese.

Fish Ravioli

PREPARATION TIME: 30 minutes	
COOKING TIME: 30 minutes	
OVEN: 180°C, 350°F, Gas Mark 4	
SERVES: 4 people	

Dough:
275g (9oz) strong plain flour
Pinch of salt
3 eggs

Filling:
*225g (8oz) sole fillets, or other flat
   fish, skinned and boned*
2 tbsps breadcrumbs
2 eggs, beaten
1 spring onion, finely chopped
1 slice of onion
1 slice of lemon
6 peppercorns
1 bay leaf
1 tbsp lemon juice
300ml (½ pint) water

Lemon sauce:
30g (1oz) butter or margarine
30g (1oz) flour
*300ml (½ pint) strained cooking
   liquid from fish*
2 tbsps double cream
2 tbsps lemon juice
Salt
Pepper

To make filling:
Pre-heat oven. Wash and dry fish. Place in oven-proof dish with slice of onion, slice of lemon, peppercorns, bay leaf, lemon juice and water. Cover and cook in oven for 20 minutes. Remove fish from liquid, and allow to drain. Strain liquid, and set aside. When fish is cool, beat with the back of a spoon to a pulp. Add eggs, breadcrumbs and spring onion, and salt and pepper to taste. Mix well.

This page: Fish Ravioli.

**Facing page: Spaghetti
Bolognese (top) and Pasta
Spirals with Creamy Parsley
Sauce (bottom).**

Pasta Spirals with Creamy Parsley Sauce

PREPARATION TIME: 5 minutes	
COOKING TIME: 15 minutes	

300g (10oz) pasta spirals
30g (1oz) butter or margarine
15g (½oz) flour
300ml (½ pint) milk
1 tbsp chopped parsley
1 tbsp lemon juice, or ½ tbsp vinegar

Heat butter in pan; when melted, stir in flour. Cook for 1 minute. Remove from heat, and gradually stir in milk. Return to heat, and stir continuously until boiling. Cook for 2 minutes. Meanwhile, cook pasta spirals in lots of boiling salted water for 10 minutes, or until tender but still firm. Rinse in hot water, and drain well. Just before serving, add lemon juice and parsley to sauce, and pour over pasta. Serve immediately.

Spaghetti Bolognese

PREPARATION TIME: 10 minutes	
COOKING TIME: 1 hour 15 minutes	

300g (10oz) spaghetti
30g (1oz) butter or margarine
15ml (1 tbsp) olive oil
2 onions, peeled and chopped finely
225g (8oz) minced beef
1 carrot, scraped and chopped finely
1 115g (4oz) can tomato purée
300ml (½ pint) brown stock
30ml (2 tbsps) sherry
Salt and pepper
Parmesan cheese, grated

Heat the butter and oil in a pan and fry the onions and carrot slowly until soft. Increase heat and add the minced beef. Fry for a few minutes, then stir, cooking until meat is

To make dough:

Sift flour into a bowl. Make a well in the centre, and add the eggs. Work the flour and eggs together with a spoon, and then knead by hand, until a smooth dough is formed. Leave to rest for 15 minutes. Lightly flour board, and roll out dough thinly into a rectangle. Cut dough in half. Shape the filling into small balls, and set them about 4cm (1½″) apart on one half of the dough. Place the other half on top, and cut with a ravioli cutter or small pastry cutter. Seal the edges. Cook in batches in a large, wide pan with plenty of boiling salted water until tender – about 8 minutes. Remove carefully with a perforated spoon. Meanwhile, make sauce.

To make sauce:

Melt butter in pan. Stir in flour, and cook for 30 seconds. Draw off heat, and gradually stir in liquid from cooked fish. Return to heat and bring to boil. Simmer for 4 minutes, stirring continuously. Add cream and mix well. Season to taste. Remove from heat, and gradually stir in lemon juice. Do not reboil.

Pour sauce over ravioli and serve immediately.

Ravioli with Ricotta Cheese

PREPARATION TIME: 30 minutes	
COOKING TIME: 20 minutes	
SERVES: 4 people	

Dough:
275g (9oz) strong plain flour
Pinch of salt
3 eggs

Filling:
30g (1oz) butter or margarine
225g (8oz) ricotta cheese
60g (2oz) Parmesan cheese, grated
1 egg yolk
2 tbsps chopped parsley
Salt
Pepper

Tomato sauce:
400g (14oz) can plum tomatoes
1 tsp basil
15ml (1 tbsp) olive oil
30g (1oz) bacon
15ml (1 tbsp) double cream
1 small onion, peeled and chopped
1 bay leaf
1 tbsp flour
Salt
Pepper

To make filling:

Beat the butter to a cream, add egg yolk, and blend well. Beat ricotta cheese to a cream, and add butter-egg mixture gradually until smooth. Add Parmesan cheese and parsley, and salt and pepper to taste. Set aside.

To make dough:

Sift flour in a bowl. Make a well in the centre, and add the eggs. Work flour and eggs together with a spoon, and then knead by hand, until a smooth dough is formed. Leave to rest for 15 minutes. Lightly flour board, and roll dough out thinly into a rectangle. Cut dough in half. Shape the filling into small balls and set them about 4cm (1½″) apart on one half of the dough. Place the other half on top and cut with a ravioli cutter or small pastry cutter. Seal the edges. Cook in batches in a large, wide pan with plenty of boiling salted water until tender – about 8 minutes. Remove carefully with a perforated spoon. Meanwhile, make sauce.

To make sauce:

Heat oil, and fry bacon and onion until golden. Add bay leaf and basil, and stir in flour. Cook for 1 minute, draw off heat, and add tomatoes gradually, stirring continuously. Add salt and pepper to taste. Return to heat and bring to boil. Cook for 5 minutes, then push through a sieve. Stir in cream, and adjust seasoning.

Pour sauce over ravioli. Serve immediately.

Wholemeal Spaghetti with Walnut and Parsley

PREPARATION TIME: 10 minutes	
COOKING TIME: 10 minutes	

300g (10oz) wholemeal spaghetti
4 tbsps parsley
2 tbsps walnuts
60ml (4 tbsps) olive oil
2 cloves garlic, peeled
Salt and pepper
3 tbsps grated Parmesan or pecorino cheese

Fry garlic gently in oil for 2 minutes. Set oil aside to cool. Wash parsley and remove stalks. Finely chop parsley, walnuts and garlic in a food processor with a metal blade, or in a blender. When chopped well, add cooled oil in a thin stream. Turn mixture into a bowl, mix in grated cheese, and add salt and pepper to taste. Cook spaghetti in a large pan of boiling salted water for 10 minutes or until tender but still firm. Drain. Serve with sauce tossed through. Serve with a side dish of grated Parmesan or pecorino cheese.

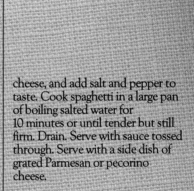

Tagliatelle with Bacon and Tomato Sauce

PREPARATION TIME: 15 minutes	
COOKING TIME: 15 minutes	

300g (10oz) red tagliatelle
1 onion, peeled and finely chopped
6 rashers of bacon, rind removed, and cut into strips

400g (14oz) can plum tomatoes,
  drained, seeds removed, and
  chopped roughly
2 tbsps chopped parsley
15ml (1 tbsp) olive oil
1 tbsp dry basil
60g (2oz) pecorino cheese, grated
Salt and pepper

Heat oil in pan. Add onion and
bacon, and cook over gentle heat
until onion is transparent but not
coloured. Add parsley, basil and
tomato. Simmer gently for
5 minutes, stirring occasionally.
Add salt and pepper to taste.
Meanwhile, cook tagliatelle in a
large pan with plenty of boiling
salted water. Cook for about
10 minutes, unil tender but still
firm. Drain and return to the pan.
Add sauce and toss through. Serve
with grated pecorino cheese.

**Tagliatelle with Bacon and
Tomato Sauce (left) and
Wholemeal Spaghetti with
Walnut and Parsley (below).**

Pasta Shells with Gorgonzola Cheese Sauce

PREPARATION TIME: 5 minutes

COOKING TIME: 15 minutes

175g (6oz) gorgonzola cheese
60ml (4 tbsps) milk
30g (1oz) butter or margarine
45ml (3 tbsps) double cream
300g (10oz) shell pasta
Salt
Parmesan cheese, grated

Heat gorgonzola cheese, milk and butter gently in a pan. Stir to a sauce with a wooden spoon. Stir in double cream. Add salt if necessary. Meanwhile, cook shells in plenty of boiling salted water for 10 minutes, or until shells are tender but still firm. Drain, shaking colander to remove excess water. Add shells to hot sauce and toss to coat well. Serve immediately with grated Parmesan cheese on the side.

Meat Ravioli

PREPARATION TIME: 30 minutes

COOKING TIME: 30 minutes

SERVES: 4 people

Dough:
275g (9oz) strong plain flour
Pinch of salt
3 eggs

Filling:
60g (2oz) butter or margarine
225g (8oz) minced beef
115g (4oz) cooked spinach, chopped
2 tbsps breadcrumbs
2 eggs, beaten
75ml (5 tbsps) red wine
1 onion, peeled and grated
1 clove garlic, crushed
Salt
Pepper

Sauce:
400g (14oz) can plum tomatoes
1 small onion, peeled and grated
1 small carrot, diced finely
1 bay leaf
3 parsley stalks
Salt
Pepper

60g (2oz) Parmesan cheese, grated

To make filling:
Heat butter in pan. Add garlic and onion, and fry gently for 1 minute. Add minced beef, and fry until browned. Add red wine, and salt

and pepper to taste, and cook uncovered for 15 minutes. Strain juices and reserve them for sauce. Allow to cool. Add breadcrumbs, chopped spinach, and beaten eggs to bind. Adjust salt and pepper to taste.

To make dough:
Sift flour in a bowl. Make a well in the centre and add the eggs. Work flour and eggs together with a spoon, then knead by hand, until a smooth dough is formed. Leave dough to rest for 15 minutes. Lightly flour board, and roll out dough thinly into a rectangle. Cut dough in half. Shape the filling into small balls, and set them about 4cm (1½″) apart on one half of the dough. Place the other half on top, and cut with a ravioli cutter or small pastry cutter. Seal the edges. Cook in batches in a large, wide pan with plenty of boiling salted

This page: Pasta Shells with Gorgonzola Cheese Sauce (top) and Spaghetti Amatriciana (bottom).

Facing page: Spinach Ravioli (top) and Meat Ravioli (bottom).

water until tender – about 8 minutes. Remove carefully with a perforated spoon. Meanwhile, make sauce.

To make sauce:
Put all ingredients in a saucepan. Add juice from cooked meat, and bring to boil. Simmer for 10 minutes. Push through a sieve, and return smooth sauce to pan. Adjust seasoning.

Put ravioli in a warm dish and cover with tomato sauce. Serve immediately, with grated Parmesan cheese.

Spaghetti Amatriciana

PREPARATION TIME: 10 minutes

COOKING TIME: 20 minutes

300g (10oz) spaghetti
1 onion, peeled and chopped finely
6 rashers bacon, rind removed, and
   cut into strips
1 400g (14oz) can plum tomatoes,
   drained, seeds removed, and
   chopped roughly
1 red chilli, seeds removed, and
   chopped finely
30ml (2 tbsps) olive oil
60g (2oz) pecorino cheese, grated

Heat oil in pan. Add onion and bacon, and cook over gentle heat until onion is soft but not coloured. Drain off surplus fat. Add tomato and chilli. Stir. Simmer gently for 5 minutes, stirring occasionally. Meanwhile, cook spaghetti in lots of boiling salted water for about 10 minutes, or until tender but still firm. Drain and return to pan. Add sauce and stir through. Serve with grated pecorino cheese.

Carrettiera with Pasta Rings

PREPARATION TIME: 5 minutes

COOKING TIME: 15 minutes

SERVES: 4 people

300g (10oz) pasta rings
200g (7oz) can tuna fish, flaked
115g (4oz) mushrooms, cleaned and
   sliced
30g (1oz) butter or margarine

Heat butter in pan, and cook mushrooms. Add tuna to warm through. Meanwhile, cook pasta in plenty of boiling salted water for 10 minutes, or until tender but still firm. Rinse under hot water. Drain well. Pour over mushroom and tuna, and toss together. Serve immediately.

Hare Sauce with Wholemeal Spaghetti

PREPARATION TIME: 10 minutes

COOKING TIME: 1 hour 15 minutes

SERVES: 4 people

300g (10oz) wholemeal spaghetti
225g (8oz) hare, cut into small pieces
115g (4oz) streaky bacon rashers, rind
   removed, and diced
2 onions, peeled and sliced
1 clove garlic, crushed
30ml (2 tbsps) olive oil
½ tsp oregano
15g (½ oz) flour
150ml (¼ pint) red wine

Heat oil in heavy pan. Lightly brown hare pieces. Remove hare pieces and put aside. Add onion, bacon, garlic and oregano to oil,

Ravioli with Ricotta Cheese (above), Brasciole with Tagliatelle (right) and Hare Sauce with Wholemeal Spaghetti (top right).

and fry until lightly coloured. Draw off heat, and stir in flour with a metal spoon. Return to heat and cook for 2 minutes. Remove from heat, and add wine, and return to heat, stirring until boiling. Add hare, cover pan, and simmer gently for about 1 hour, until hare is tender. Add salt and pepper to taste. When sauce is ready, cook spaghetti in lots of boiling salted water for about 10 minutes, or until tender but still firm. Rinse in hot water, and drain. Serve with hare sauce on top. Serve immediately.

Brasciole with Tagliatelle

PREPARATION TIME: 15 minutes

COOKING TIME: 25 minutes

SERVES: 4 people

225g (8oz) tagliatelle
4 veal steaks
4 thin slices ham
4 tbsps grated Parmesan cheese
30g (1oz) butter or margarine
400g (14oz) can plum tomatoes
Salt
Pepper

Push tomatoes and their juice through a sieve. Pound veal steaks out thinly. Place a slice of ham on the top of each steak. Sprinkle a tablespoon of the Parmesan cheese over each steak, and freshly-ground black pepper. Roll up, and tie gently with string at each end and in the middle. Heat butter in a pan, and add veal rolls. Cook gently until lightly browned all over. Add puréed tomatoes, and cover. Cook for 15 minutes. Meanwhile, cook tagliatelle in plenty of boiling salted water for 10 minutes, or until tender but still firm. Rinse in hot water, and drain. Cut veal rolls into 2.5cm (1″) rounds. Toss tagliatelle together with tomato sauce, and top with veal rolls and grated Parmesan cheese. Serve immediately.

Tagliatelle with Garlic and Oil

PREPARATION TIME: 5 minutes

COOKING TIME: 10 minutes

300g (10oz) green tagliatelle
150ml (¼ pint) olive oil
3 cloves garlic, crushed
2 tbsps chopped parsley
Salt and pepper

Cook the tagliatelle in lots of boiling salted water for 10 minutes, or until tender but still firm, stirring occasionally. Meanwhile, make the sauce. Heat the oil in a pan and, when warm, add peeled, crushed garlic. Fry gently until golden brown. Add chopped parsley, and salt and pepper to taste. Drain tagliatelle. Add sauce, and toss to coat well. Serve hot.

Farfalle with Tomato Sauce

PREPARATION TIME: 10 minutes

COOKING TIME: 30 minutes

300g (10oz) farfalle
2 400g (14oz) can plum tomatoes, chopped
15ml (1 tbsp) olive oil
1 onion, peeled and sliced
2 cloves garlic, crushed
½ tsp dry basil
Salt and pepper
2 tbsps chopped fresh basil or chopped parsley
Parmesan cheese, grated

Heat oil in a deep pan. Add garlic and onion, and cook until softened. Add dry basil, and cook for 30 seconds. Add undrained tomatoes; season with salt and pepper. Bring to the boil, reduce heat, and simmer, uncovered, for about 20 minutes, or until sauce is reduced by half. Meanwhile, cook

the pasta in a large pan of boiling salted water, until tender but still firm – about 10 minutes. Rinse in hot water, and drain well. Put sauce through a sieve, and stir in the fresh parsley or basil. Toss sauce through pasta. Serve with grated Parmesan cheese. Serve immediately.

Pasta Shells with Mushroom Sauce

PREPARATION TIME: 5 minutes

COOKING TIME: 15 minutes

300g (10oz) pasta shells
225g (8oz) button mushrooms
30g (1oz) butter or margarine
15g (½oz) flour
600ml (1 pint) milk
Salt and pepper

Rinse the mushrooms and chop them roughly. Melt butter in a saucepan and add mushrooms. Fry for 5 minutes, stirring occasionally. Stir in the flour and cook for 1 minute. Draw off the heat, and add milk gradually, stirring continuously. Bring to the boil and cook for 3 minutes. Season with salt and pepper. Meanwhile, cook

This page: Tagliatelle with Garlic and Oil (top) and Spaghetti with Basil Sauce (Pesto) (bottom).

Facing page: Pasta Shells with Mushroom Sauce (top) and Farfalle with Tomato Sauce (bottom).

the pasta shells in lots of boiling salted water for 10 minutes, or until tender but still firm. Rinse in hot water and drain well. Place in a warmed serving dish, and pour over mushroom sauce. Serve immediately.

Tortellini

PREPARATION TIME: 30 minutes
COOKING TIME: 15 minutes
SERVES: 4 people

Dough:
300g (10oz) strong plain flour
Pinch of salt
3 eggs
15ml (1 tbsp) water
15ml (1 tbsp) oil

Filling:
1 cooked chicken breast, finely diced
2 spinach leaves, stalks removed, cooked and chopped finely
30g (1oz) ham, finely diced
1 tbsp grated Parmesan cheese
30g (1oz) cream cheese
1 egg, beaten
Salt
Pepper

Sauce:
300ml (½ pint) single cream
60g (2oz) mushrooms, cleaned and sliced
60g (2oz) Parmesan cheese, grated
1 tbsp chopped parsley
Salt
Pepper

To make filling:
Beat the cream cheese until soft and smooth. Add chicken, ham, spinach and Parmesan cheese, and mix well. Add egg gradually, and salt and pepper to taste. Set aside.

To make dough:
Sift flour and salt onto a board. Make a well in the centre. Mix water, oil and lightly-beaten egg together, and gradually pour into well, working in the flour with the other hand, a little at a time. Continue until the mixture comes together in a firm ball of dough. Knead on a lightly-floured board for 5 minutes, or until smooth and elastic. Put into a bowl, cover with a cloth, and let stand for 15 minutes. Roll dough out on a lightly-floured board as thinly as possible. Using a 5cm (2") cutter, cut out rounds. Put ½ teaspoon of filling into the centre of each round. Fold in half, pressing edges together firmly. Wrap around forefinger, and press ends together. Cook in batches in a large pan, in plenty of boiling salted water for about 10 minutes until tender, stirring occasionally.

To make sauce:
Meanwhile, gently heat cream in a pan. Add mushrooms, Parmesan cheese, parsley, and salt and pepper to taste. Gently cook for 3 minutes.

Toss sauce together with tortellini. Serve immediately, sprinkled with parsley.

Pasta Shells with Walnuts and Cream Cheese

PREPARATION TIME: 5 minutes
COOKING TIME: 15 minutes

300g (10oz) pasta shells
15ml (1 tbsp) olive oil
1 clove garlic, crushed
1 tbsp oregano
30g (1oz) butter or margarine
60ml (4 tbsps) milk
115g (4oz) packet cream cheese
115g (4oz) walnuts, chopped very finely (keep a few aside to decorate)
60ml (4 tbsps) cream
Parmesan cheese, grated
Salt and pepper

Heat oil in a pan. Add crushed garlic and oregano, and cook for 1 minute. Add butter, cream cheese, chopped walnuts, and salt and pepper to taste. Stir, and leave to simmer gently for 5 minutes. Meanwhile, cook pasta shells in plenty of boiling salted water for 10 minutes, or until shells are tender but still firm. Drain in a colander, shaking to remove any trapped water. Put into warmed serving dish. Remove sauce from heat; add cream, and stir. Pour over shells, and toss to coat evenly. Garnish with walnut halves. Serve immediately with grated Parmesan cheese.

Spinach Ravioli

PREPARATION TIME: 30 minutes
COOKING TIME: 20 minutes
SERVES: 4 people

Dough:
275g (9oz) strong plain flour
Pinch of salt
3 eggs

Filling:
225g (8oz) cooked spinach
30g (1oz) butter or margarine
60g (2oz) Parmesan cheese, grated
Pinch of grated nutmeg
1 egg, beaten
Salt
Pepper

Cream cheese sauce:
30g (1oz) butter or margarine
15g (½ oz) flour
300ml (½ pint) milk
1 tsp French mustard
2 tbsps grated Parmesan cheese

To make filling:
Chop spinach and heat in a pan. Beat butter into spinach. Add Parmesan cheese, nutmeg, and salt and freshly-ground black pepper to taste. Finally mix in the beaten egg well.

To make dough:
Sift flour in a bowl; make a well in the centre, and add the eggs. Work flour and eggs together with a spoon, and then knead by hand, until a smooth dough is formed. Leave to rest for 15 minutes. Lightly flour board, and roll out dough thinly into a rectangle. Cut dough in half. Shape the filling into small balls, and set them about 4cm (1½") apart on one half of the dough. Place the other half on top, and cut with a ravioli cutter or small pastry cutter. Seal the edges.

Cook in batches in a large, wide pan with plenty of boiling salted water until tender – about 8 minutes. Remove carefully with a perforated spoon. Meanwhile, make sauce.

To make sauce:
Heat butter in pan. Stir in flour and cook for 30 seconds. Draw off heat, and stir milk in gradually. Bring to boil and simmer for 3 minutes, stirring continuously. Add mustard, and half the cheese, and seasoning to taste.

Pour sauce over ravioli, and serve immediately with remaining cheese sprinkled over the top.

Spaghetti with Basil Sauce (Pesto)

PREPARATION TIME: 5 minutes
COOKING TIME: 15 minutes

300g (10oz) spaghetti
2 cups fresh basil leaves

Tagliatelle with Butter and Cheese (top) and Pasta Shells with Walnuts and Cream Sauce (right).

2 tbsps pine nuts
75ml (5 tbsps) olive oil
2 cloves garlic, peeled
Salt and pepper
3 tbsps Parmesan or pecorino cheese, grated

Garnish:
Fresh basil

Wash basil and remove leaves, discarding stems. Heat 1 tablespoon of oil over a low temperature. Add garlic and pine nuts, and cook until pine nuts are a light golden brown. Drain. Finely chop basil leaves, pine nuts and garlic in a food processor with a metal blade, or in a blender. When smooth, add remaining oil in a thin stream, blending continuously. Turn mixture into a bowl; mix in grated cheese, and add salt and pepper to taste. Meanwhile, cook spaghetti in a large pan of boiling salted water for 10 minutes, or until just tender. Drain, and serve with basil sauce tossed through. Serve with side dish of grated cheese. Garnish with fresh basil.

Penne with Spicy Chilli Sauce

PREPARATION TIME: 15 minutes

COOKING TIME: 40 minutes

300g (10oz) penne
1 onion, peeled and chopped
400g (14oz) can plum tomatoes
2 red chillies, seeds removed, and chopped finely
2 cloves garlic, crushed
15ml (1 tbsp) olive oil
115g (4oz) bacon, rind removed, and diced
60g (2oz) pecorino cheese, grated
2 spring onions, chopped
Salt and pepper

Garnish:
4 spring onions (cut into 5cm [2 inch] strips. Keeping one end intact, cut into strips. Soak in chilled water until the flower has opened).

Chop tomatoes, removing seeds by straining juice. Heat oil in a pan, and fry garlic, onion and bacon gently for 10 minutes. Add tomato, chillies and chopped spring onions, and half the cheese, and salt and pepper to taste. Cook, uncovered, for 20 minutes. 10 minutes before sauce is ready, cook the penne in lots of boiling salted water for 10 minutes, or until tender but still firm. Rinse under hot water, and drain well. Put into a warmed serving dish, and toss together with half the sauce. Pour remaining sauce on top, and garnish with spring onion flowers, and remaining cheese if desired. Serve at once.

Tagliatelle with Butter and Cheese

PREPARATION TIME: 5 minutes

COOKING TIME: 15 minutes

300g (10oz) tagliatelle – 100g (3½oz) each yellow, green and red tagliatelle
90g (3oz) butter
60g (2oz) Parmesan cheese, grated
90ml (6 tbsps) double cream
Salt and pepper

Cook the tagliatelle in a large pan of boiling salted water for 10 minutes, or until just tender. Drain. Meanwhile, put the butter and

cream in a pan, and stir over a low heat until butter has melted. Remove from heat, add half the grated cheese, and salt and pepper to taste. Stir into tagliatelle and serve immediately with remaining cheese on top.

Pasta Spirals with Peas and Tomatoes

PREPARATION TIME: 5 minutes

COOKING TIME: 15 minutes

300g (10oz) pasta spirals
350g (12oz) peas
1 tsp sugar
400g (14oz) can plum tomatoes, chopped
1 tsp basil
60g (2oz) butter or margarine
Salt and pepper

Cook pasta spirals in plenty of boiling salted water for 10 minutes or until tender. Drain. Meanwhile,

cook peas in boiling water with a pinch of salt and a teaspoon of sugar. Melt butter in a pan. Add basil, and cook for 30 seconds. Add tomatoes and their juice. When hot, add pasta spirals and peas, and salt and pepper to taste. Toss together. Serve immediately.

Spaghetti with Egg, Bacon and Mushroom

PREPARATION TIME: 10 minutes

COOKING TIME: 15 minutes

300g (10oz) spaghetti
225g (8oz) mushrooms, sliced
115g (4oz) bacon rashers, rind removed, and diced
60g (2oz) butter or margarine
60g (2oz) Parmesan cheese, grated
2 eggs, hard-boiled and chopped finely
1 tbsp chopped parsley
Salt and pepper

Melt half the butter in a frying-pan. Add mushrooms and bacon, and cook for 10 minutes over a moderate heat, until bacon is crisp. Meanwhile, cook the spaghetti in lots of boiling salted water until tender but still firm – about 10 minutes. Drain. Return to pan. Add rest of butter, salt and lots of freshly-ground black pepper, and the mushroom and bacon. Toss together. Serve with hard-boiled eggs sprinkled on top, and parsley if desired. Serve grated Parmesan cheese separately.

This page: Pasta Spirals with Peas and Tomatoes.

Facing page: Spaghetti with Egg, Bacon and Mushroom (top) and Penne with Spicy Chilli Sauce (bottom).

Salads and Stuffed Vegetables

celery to macaroni. Pour over dressing, and toss together.

Niçoise Salad

PREPARATION TIME: 15 minutes

COOKING TIME: 15 minutes

SERVES: 4 people

225g (8oz) penne
3 tomatoes, quartered
115g (4oz) French beans, cooked
½ cucumber, cut into batons
200g (7oz) can tuna fish, drained and flaked
12 black olives, halved, with stones removed
45g (1½oz) can anchovy fillets, drained, and soaked in milk if desired
120ml (4 fl oz) bottled French dressing

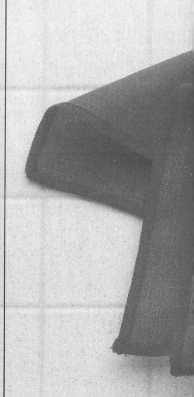

Bean Salad

PREPARATION TIME: 10 minutes

COOKING TIME: 15 minutes

SERVES: 4 people

225g (8oz) macaroni
425g (15oz) can red kidney beans, drained

60g (2oz) bacon, rind removed, and sliced
1 onion, peeled and chopped
2 sticks celery, sliced diagonally
15-30ml (1-2 tbsps) wine vinegar
45-60ml (3-4 tbsps) olive oil
1 tsp chopped parsley
Salt
Pepper

Cook macaroni in plenty of salted boiling water for 10 minutes, or until tender but still firm. Rinse in cold water and drain well.
Heat frying pan, and sauté bacon in its own fat until crisp. Add onion, and cook until soft. Mix vinegar, oil and parsley, and season well. Add bacon, onion, kidney beans and

Nicoise Salad (far left), Bean Salad (left) and Tuna and Tomato Salad (below).

Cook penne in lots of boiling salted water until tender but still firm. Rinse in cold water; drain, and leave to dry. Put flaked tuna in the base of a salad dish. Toss pasta together with tomatoes, cucumber, French beans, olives, and anchovies, and then pour over French dressing. Mix together well.

Tuna and Tomato Salad

PREPARATION TIME: 10 minutes

COOKING TIME: 15 minutes

SERVES: 4 people

225g (8oz) pasta shells
200g (7oz) can tuna fish, flaked
6 tomatoes
1 tbsp fresh chopped basil or
*   marjoram, or 1 tsp dried basil or*
*   oregano*
90ml (6 tbsps) French dressing

Mix herbs with French dressing. Cook pasta shells in a large saucepan of boiling salted water until tender – about 10 minutes. Rinse with cold water, and drain, shaking off excess water. Toss with 3 tablespoons of French dressing. Leave to cool. Meanwhile, slice enough of the tomatoes to arrange around the outside of the serving-dish. Chop the rest, and pour the remaining French dressing over them, and place in the centre of the dish. Add tuna to the pasta shells, and toss gently. Serve in the centre of the dish over the chopped tomatoes.

Stuffed Aubergine (Eggplant)

PREPARATION TIME: 15 minutes

COOKING TIME: 1 hour

OVEN: 180°C, 350°F, Gas Mark 4
         200°C, 400°F, Gas Mark 6

4 small or 2 large aubergines
60g (2oz) soup macaroni
200g (7oz) bacon, rind removed, and
*   diced*
1 green pepper, cored and diced
1 yellow pepper, cored and diced
2 tomatoes, skin removed, chopped
*   and seeds removed*
30g (1oz) butter
½ tsp chilli powder
1 tbsp tomato purée
1 small onion, peeled and chopped
1 clove garlic, crushed
60g (2oz) Gruyère or Cheddar
*   cheese, grated*
1 tbsp breadcrumbs
Salt and pepper

Cook macaroni in plenty of boiling, salted water for 10 minutes, or until tender but still firm. Rinse in cold water, and drain well. Wrap aubergines in baking foil, and bake in a moderate oven (180°C, 350°F, Gas Mark 4) for 30 minutes. Cut aubergines in half lengthways. Scoop out the pulp, leaving 1.5cm (½ inch) of thickness on the skin. Chop pulp. Heat butter in a pan. Add onion and garlic, and cook until transparent. Add bacon and peppers and fry for 5 minutes. Then add aubergine pulp, tomato, tomato purée, chilli powder, and salt and pepper. Cook a further 3

minutes. Stir in macaroni, and fill the scooped-out aubergine halves with the mixture. Top with grated cheese and breadcrumbs, and brown under a grill or in a quick oven (200°C, 400°F, Gas Mark 6). Serve immediately.

Gianfottere Salad

PREPARATION TIME: 40 minutes

COOKING TIME: 30 minutes

SERVES: 4 people

225g (8oz) pasta spirals
1 aubergine (egg plant)

1 courgette (zucchini)
1 red pepper
1 green pepper
2 tomatoes
1 onion
60ml (4 tbsps) olive oil
1 clove garlic
Salt
Pepper

This page: Gianfottere Salad.

Facing page: Stuffed Aubergine (Eggplant).

Cut aubergine into 1cm (½") slices. Sprinkle with salt and leave for 30 minutes. Skin the tomatoes by putting them into boiling water for 20 seconds, and then rinsing in cold water, and peeling skins off. Chop roughly. Cut courgette into 1cm (½") slices. Remove cores and seeds from peppers, and chop roughly. Peel and chop onion. Heat 45ml (3 tbsps) olive oil in pan, and fry onion gently until transparent, but not coloured. Meanwhile, rinse salt from aubergine, and pat dry with absorbent paper. Chop roughly. Add aubergine, courgette, peppers, tomatoes and garlic to onion, and fry gently for 20 minutes. Season with salt and pepper. Allow to cool. Meanwhile, cook pasta spirals in a lot of boiling salted water for 10 minutes, or until tender but still firm. Rinse in cold water and drain well, and toss in remaining 15ml (1 tbsp) olive oil. Toss vegetables together with pasta spirals.

Stuffed Courgettes (Zucchini)

PREPARATION TIME: 15 minutes

COOKING TIME: 30 minutes

OVEN: 200°C, 400°F, Gas Mark 7

4 courgettes
60g (2oz) soup pasta
2 tomatoes, skin removed, chopped, and seeds removed
30g (1oz) butter or margarine
115g (4oz) minced beef
1 small onion, peeled and chopped
2 cloves garlic, crushed
60g (2oz) Gruyère or Cheddar cheese, grated
1 tbsp breadcrumbs
1 tsp tomato purée
Salt and pepper

Cook pasta in lots of boiling salted water for 5 minutes or until tender. Rinse in cold water and drain well. Meanwhile, put courgettes in a pan and cover with cold water. Bring to the boil and cook gently for 3 minutes. Rinse under cold water. Cut courgettes in half lengthways. Carefully scoop out the pulp, leaving 1.5cm (½ inch) thickness on skin. Chop pulp. Heat butter in a frying-pan. Add garlic and onion, and fry gently until transparent. Increase heat and add minced beef. Cook for 5 minutes, turning often until meat is well browned. Stir in tomato purée and salt and pepper to taste. Add courgette pulp, tomatoes and pasta, and cook for 2 minutes. Spoon into courgette shells. Sprinkle top with grated cheese and breadcrumbs, and

brown under a hot grill or in a quick oven. Serve immediately.

Stuffed Tomatoes

PREPARATION TIME: 10 minutes

COOKING TIME: 20 minutes

OVEN: 180°C, 350°F, Gas Mark 4

4 large ripe tomatoes
450g (1lb) fresh spinach
¼ tsp grated nutmeg
30g (1oz) butter, creamed
60g (2oz) soup pasta
15ml (1 tbsp) double cream
1 clove garlic, crushed
15g (½oz) Gruyère or Cheddar cheese, grated
4 anchovy fillets, sliced
Salt and pepper

Cut tops off tomatoes, and carefully scoop out the insides with a teaspoon. Wash spinach well and remove stalks. Cook gently in a large saucepan, without added water, until spinach is soft. Chop very finely, or blend in a food processor. Meanwhile, cook pasta for 5 minutes, or until tender. Rinse and drain well. Mix with the spinach. Add butter, cream, nutmeg and garlic, and season well. Fill each tomato and top with cheese and anchovy fillets. Bake in a moderate oven for 10 minutes. Serve immediately.

Mushroom Salad

PREPARATION TIME: 1 hour 10 minutes

COOKING TIME: 15 minutes

SERVES: 4 people

225g (8oz) farfalle (pasta butterflies/ bows)
225g (8oz) mushrooms (button or cup), sliced
75ml (5 tbsps) olive oil
Juice of 2 lemons
1 tsp fresh chopped basil
1 tsp fresh chopped parsley
Salt
Pepper

Mix oil together with lemon juice and fresh herbs. Put the sliced mushrooms into a bowl, and pour over 60ml (4 tbsps) of the dressing. Leave for 1 hour. Cook the pasta in a large saucepan of boiling salted water for 10 minutes, or until tender. Rinse in cold water, and drain. Toss with the rest of the dressing, and leave to cool. Fold mushrooms and pasta together gently, adding salt and freshly-ground black pepper to taste. Sprinkle with parsley.

Prawn Salad

PREPARATION TIME: 10 minutes

COOKING TIME: 15 minutes

SERVES: 4 people

225g (8oz) pasta shells
225g (8oz) prawns or shrimps, shelled and de-veined
150ml (¼ pint) mayonnaise
Juice of 1 lemon
1 tsp paprika
Salt
Pepper
1 lettuce
1 cucumber, sliced

Cook the pasta in plenty of boiling salted water for 10 minutes, or until tender. Drain, and rinse under cold water. Shake off excess water; put into a bowl, and pour over lemon juice. Leave to cool. Mix paprika into mayonnaise. Add to prawns, and toss. Arrange a bed of lettuce leaves and sliced cucumber in a dish, and pile pasta in centre. Pile prawns on top.
(This can also be made with flaked crab meat or salmon).

Stuffed Courgettes (Zucchini) (above right) and Stuffed Tomatoes (top).

Prawn Salad (left) and Mushroom Salad (far left).

Curried Prawn Salad

PREPARATION TIME: 10 minutes

COOKING TIME: 20 minutes

SERVES: 4 people

225g (8oz) soup pasta
225g (8oz) prawns or shrimps,
*   shelled and de-veined*
1 tsp paprika
Juice of ½ a lemon
1 dsp curry powder
1 tsp tomato purée
30ml (2 tbsps) olive oil
1 small onion, peeled and chopped
1 clove garlic, crushed
150ml (¼ pint) water
2 slices lemon
1 tsp apricot jam
300ml (½ pint) mayonnaise
Salt
Pepper

Heat oil, and fry garlic and onion gently until soft but not coloured. Add curry powder and paprika, and cook for 2 minutes. Stir in tomato purée and water. Add lemon slices, and salt and pepper to taste. Cook slowly for 10 minutes; stir in jam, and bring to the boil, simmering for 2 minutes. Strain and leave to cool. Add mayonnaise. Meanwhile, cook pasta in plenty of boiling salted water for 10 minutes, or until tender but still firm. Rinse under cold water and drain well. Toss in lemon juice, and put in serving-dish. Arrange prawns on top, and pour over curry sauce. Toss well. Sprinkle with paprika.

Courgette (Zucchini) Salad

PREPARATION TIME: 15 minutes

COOKING TIME: 15 minutes

SERVES: 4 people

225g (8oz) elbow macaroni
4 courgettes, sliced thinly
2 tomatoes, chopped
8 stuffed green olives, sliced
90ml (6 tbsps) French dressing

Cook pasta in lots of boiling salted water for 10 minutes, or until tender but still firm. Rinse in cold water, and drain well. Mix with 3 tablespoons French dressing. Leave to cool. Meanwhile, cook the courgettes gently in boiling, lightly-salted water, until just tender but still crisp. Drain, and flush with cold water. Leave to cool. Mix together pasta, courgettes, tomatoes and stuffed olives, and 3 tablespoons French dressing. Serve chilled.

Mexican Chicken Salad

PREPARATION TIME: 10 minutes

COOKING TIME: 15 minutes

SERVES: 4 people

225g (8oz) soup pasta shells
225g (8oz) cooked chicken, shredded
200g (7oz) can sweetcorn kernels,
*   drained*
1 stick celery, sliced
1 red pepper, cored, seeds removed,
*   and diced*
1 green pepper, cored, seeds removed,
*   and diced*

Dressing:
15ml (1 tbsp) mayonnaise
30ml (2 tbsps) vinegar
Salt
Pepper

Cook pasta in plenty of boiling salted water until just tender. Drain well, and leave to cool. Meanwhile, combine mayonnaise with vinegar and salt and pepper to taste. When the pasta is cool, add chicken, sweetcorn, celery and peppers. Toss well and serve with dressing.

This page: Mexican Chicken Salad.

Facing page: Curried Prawn Salad (top) and Courgette (Zucchini) Salad (bottom).

Offal

Pasta Spirals with Kidneys in Madeira Sauce

PREPARATION TIME: 15 minutes
COOKING TIME: 30 minutes

300g (10oz) pasta spirals
225g (8oz) lambs' kidneys
1 tbsp flour
Salt and pepper
1 small onion, peeled and chopped finely
1 clove garlic, crushed
60g (2oz) butter or margarine
115g (4oz) button mushrooms, sliced
90g (3oz) bacon, rind removed, and diced
90ml (6 tbsps) Madeira wine, or dry white wine

Remove skin, fat and hard core from kidneys. Cut in half lengthways. Add salt and pepper to flour and mix well. Coat kidneys in seasoned flour. Heat butter in pan; add onion and garlic, and cook until soft and translucent. Add kidneys and brown on both sides. Add bacon and mushroom, and cook, stirring frequently, for 3 minutes. Add wine, and bring to the boil. Simmer gently for 15 minutes, or until kidneys are tender. Adjust seasoning. Meanwhile, cook the pasta spirals in plenty of boiling salted water for 10 minutes, or until tender but still firm. Rinse in hot water and drain well. Serve immediately, with kidney sauce on top.

Tagliatelle with Creamy Liver Sauce

PREPARATION TIME: 10 minutes
COOKING TIME: 15 minutes

300g (10oz) tagliatelle
60ml (4 tbsps) olive oil
2 medium onions, peeled and sliced
1 clove garlic, crushed
115g (4oz) mushrooms, sliced
450g (1lb) chicken livers, cleaned and sliced
120ml (8 tbsps) single cream
2 eggs, beaten
1 tbsp chopped parsley
Salt and pepper

In a large frying pan, cook onions and garlic gently in oil until softened. Add mushrooms and cook for 3 minutes. Add chicken livers to onions and mushrooms, and cook until lightly browned. Remove from heat and stir in cream. Return to low heat, and cook, uncovered, for further 2

Tagliatelle with Creamy Liver Sauce (left) and Pasta Spirals with Kidneys in Madeira Sauce (below).

minutes. Remove from heat, and stir in lightly beaten eggs. Season with salt and pepper to taste. Meanwhile, cook the tagliatelle in plenty of boiling salted water for

10 minutes, or until tender but still firm, stirring occasionally. Drain tagliatelle, toss in oil and black pepper. Serve sauce over tagliatelle and sprinkle with parsley.

Baked and Grilled Dishes

Cannelloni

PREPARATION TIME: 10 minutes
COOKING TIME: 1 hour
OVEN: 180°C, 350°F, Gas Mark 4
SERVES: 4 people

12 cannelloni shells
2 tbsps Parmesan cheese, grated
15ml (1 tbsp) oil

Filling:
450g (1lb) minced beef
15ml (1 tbsp) olive oil
1 onion, peeled and chopped
2 cloves garlic, crushed
225g (8oz) packet frozen spinach,
   thawed
½ tsp oregano
½ tsp basil
1 tsp tomato purée
60ml (4 tbsps) cream
1 egg, lightly beaten
Salt and pepper to taste

Tomato sauce:
15ml (1 tbsp) olive oil
1 onion, peeled and chopped
1 clove garlic, crushed
400g (14oz) can plum tomatoes
2 tbsps tomato purée
Salt
Pepper

Béchamel sauce:
1 slice of onion
3 peppercorns
1 small bay leaf
300ml (½ pint) milk
30g (1oz) butter or margarine
30g (1oz) flour
Salt
Pepper

To make filling:
Heat oil in pan, and fry garlic and onion gently until soft and transparent. Add meat and cook, stirring continuously, until well browned. Drain off any fat, add tomato purée, basil and oregano, and cook gently for 15 minutes. Add spinach, egg and cream, and salt and pepper to taste. Cook cannelloni in a large pan of boiling salted water for 15-20 minutes, until tender. Rinse in hot water and drain. Fill carefully with meat mixture, using a piping bag with a wide, plain nozzle, or a teaspoon.

To make tomato sauce:
Heat oil in pan. Add onion and garlic, and cook gently until transparent. Push tomatoes through a sieve, and add to the pan with tomato purée and salt and pepper to taste. Bring to boil, and then simmer for 5 minutes. Set aside.

To make Béchamel sauce:
Put milk in pan with onion, peppercorns and bay leaf. Heat gently for 1 minute, taking care not to boil, and set aside to cool for 5 minutes. Strain. Melt butter in

This page: **Prawn Crespelle.**

Facing page: **Cannelloni with Tomato and Cheese** (top) and **Cannelloni** (bottom).

Crespelle with Tuna (left) and
Crespelle with Chicken and
Tongue (below).

pan. Remove from heat and stir in flour. Gradually add cool milk, and bring to boil, stirring continuously, until sauce thickens. Add seasoning.

Spread tomato sauce on the base of an oven-proof dish. Lay cannelloni on top, and cover with Béchamel sauce. Sprinkle with grated cheese, and bake in a moderate oven for 30 minutes. Serve immediately.

Prawn Crespelle

PREPARATION TIME: 40 minutes

COOKING TIME: 30 minutes

OVEN: 190°C, 375°F, Gas Mark 5

SERVES: 4 people

12 crespelle:
3 eggs
115g (4oz) plain flour
Pinch of salt
200ml (8 fl oz) water
8ml (½ tbsp) olive oil
30g (1oz) butter or margarine, melted

Filling:
225g (8oz) prawns or shrimps, washed, peeled and de-veined
30g (1oz) butter or margarine
15g (½oz) flour
300ml (½ pint) milk
Juice of 1 lemon
Salt
Pepper

Garnish:
1 lemon, cut into slices

To make crespelle:
Sift flour with a pinch of salt. Break eggs into a bowl, and whisk. Add flour gradually, whisking all the time until the mixture is smooth. Add water, and stir in well. Add oil, and mix. Cover bowl with damp cloth, and leave in a cool place for 30 minutes.
Heat a crêpe pan or 19cm (7") frying pan. Grease lightly with melted butter, and put a tablespoon of batter in the centre. Roll the pan to coat the surface evenly. Fry until crespelle is brown on the underside. Loosen edge with a palette knife; turn over and brown the other side. Stack and wrap in a clean cloth until needed.

To make filling:
Heat butter in pan; stir in flour, and cook for 1 minute. Remove from heat, and gradually stir in milk. Return to heat, and bring to the boil. Allow to simmer for 3 minutes. Stir in lemon juice and add salt and pepper to taste. Add half the sauce to prawns. Place one crespelle in an oven-proof dish, and add a spoon of prawn mixture. Cover with one crespelle, and repeat, finishing with a crespelle on top. Bake in a pre-heated oven for 10 minutes. When ready to serve, cover with remaining sauce. Garnish with lemon slices. Serve immediately.

Crespelle with Chicken and Tongue

PREPARATION TIME: 40 minutes

COOKING TIME: 20 minutes

OVEN: 230°C, 450°F, Gas Mark 8

SERVES: 4 people

10 crespelle:
3 eggs
115g (4oz) plain flour
Pinch of salt
200ml (8 fl oz) water
8ml (½ tsp) olive oil
30g (1oz) butter or margarine, melted

Filling:
115g (4oz) chicken, cooked and shredded
115g (4oz) tongue, cut into strips

Béchamel sauce:
30g (1oz) butter or margarine
15g (½oz) flour
300ml (½ pint) milk
To infuse:
4 peppercorns
1 bay leaf
Slice of onion
Salt
Pepper

To make crespelle:
Sift flour with a pinch of salt. Break eggs into a bowl, and whisk. Add flour gradually, whisking all the time until the mixture is smooth. Add water and stir in well. Add oil, and mix. Cover bowl with a damp cloth, and leave in a cool place for 30 minutes.
Heat a crêpe pan, or 19cm (7") frying pan. Grease lightly with melted butter, and put a good tablespoon of batter in the centre. Roll the pan to coat the surface evenly. Fry until crespelle is brown on the underside. Loosen edge with a palette knife; turn over and brown the other side. Stack and wrap in a clean cloth until needed.

To make Béchamel sauce:
Warm milk with peppercorns, bay leaf and slice of onion. Remove from heat, and let stand for 5 minutes. Strain. Heat butter in pan. Stir in flour and cook for 1 minute. Remove from heat, and gradually stir in two-thirds (200ml) of the milk. Return to heat, and stir continuously until boiling. Simmer for 3 minutes. Add salt and pepper to taste. Put half of the sauce in a bowl, and add the chicken and tongue. Mix together. Beat remaining milk (100ml) into remaining sauce.

Lay 1 crespelle on a plate, and top with a layer of chicken and tongue. Cover with another crespelle, and continue, finishing with a crespelle.

Pour over sauce, and bake in pre-heated oven for 10 minutes. Serve immediately.

Crespelle with Tuna

PREPARATION TIME: 40 minutes

COOKING TIME: 30 minutes

SERVES: 4 people

12 crespelle:
3 eggs
115g (4oz) plain flour
Pinch of salt
200ml (8 fl oz) water
8ml (½ tbsp) olive oil
30g (1oz) butter or margarine, melted

Filling:
270g (9oz) can tuna fish, drained
3 tbsps mayonnaise
1 tbsp tomato purée

Tomato sauce:
400g (14oz) can plum tomatoes
½ tsp basil
1 clove garlic, crushed
1 onion, peeled and chopped
15g (½oz) butter or margarine
2 tbsps chopped parsley
Salt
Pepper

To make crespelle:
Sift the flour with a pinch of salt. Break eggs into a bowl, and whisk. Add flour gradually, whisking all the time, until the mixture is smooth. Stir in water, and mix oil in well. Cover bowl with a damp cloth, and leave in a cool place for 30 minutes.
Heat a crêpe pan, or 19cm (7") frying pan. Grease lightly with melted butter, and put a good tablespoon of batter in the centre. Roll the pan to coat the surface evenly. Fry until crespelle is brown on the underside. Loosen edge with a palette knife; turn over and brown on the other side. Stack and wrap in a clean cloth until needed.

To make sauce:
Heat butter in pan, and gently fry garlic and basil for 30 seconds. Add onion, and fry until transparent. Add tomatoes, and cook for 10 minutes. Push through a sieve, and return to pan. Add salt, and freshly-ground black pepper, to taste, and parsley if desired.

To make filling:
Flake tuna fish, and put into a bowl. Mix mayonnaise and tomato purée, and stir into tuna fish. Divide mixture equally between crespelle, placing mixture at one end, and rolling up. Place in an oven-proof dish. Pour over tomato sauce, and cook under a hot grill for 5 minutes. Serve immediately.

Cook the macaroni in plenty of boiling salted water for 10 minutes, or until tender but still firm. Rinse in hot water and drain well. Meanwhile, melt the butter in a pan. Stir in the flour and cook for 1 minute. Remove from heat, and gradually stir in the milk. Return to heat and bring to the boil. Simmer for 3 minutes, stirring continuously. Stir in the mustard, anchovies, and half the cheese. Season with salt and pepper to taste. Stir in the macaroni, and pour into an oven-proof dish. Sprinkle the remaining cheese over the top, and make a latticework with the remaining anchovies. Brown under a hot grill. Serve immediately.

Macaroni with Creamy Chicken Sauce

PREPARATION TIME: 5 minutes
COOKING TIME: 20 minutes
SERVES: 4 people

225g (8oz) macaroni
60g (2oz) butter or margarine
30g (1oz) flour
600ml (1 pint) milk
115g (4oz) chicken breasts
15ml (1 tbsp) olive oil
115g (4oz) Cheddar cheese, grated
Salt
Pepper

Heat oil in a frying pan, and gently fry chicken for 10 minutes, or until cooked through. When cool, shred chicken. Cook macaroni in plenty of boiling salted water for 10 minutes, or until tender but still firm. Rinse in hot water. Drain well. Meanwhile, heat the butter in a pan, and stir in the flour, and cook for 1 minute. Draw off the heat and gradually add the milk, stirring all the time. Bring the sauce to the boil, stirring continuously, and cook for 3 minutes. Add the chicken, macaroni, and salt and pepper to taste, and mix well. Pour mixture into an oven-proof dish, and sprinkle with cheese on top. Cook under a pre-heated grill until golden brown. Serve immediately.

Macaroni Cheese with Anchovies

PREPARATION TIME: 5 minutes
COOKING TIME: 15 minutes
SERVES: 4 people

225g (8oz) macaroni
60g (2oz) butter or margarine
60g (2oz) flour
600ml (1 pint) milk
½ tsp dry mustard
175g (6oz) Gruyère or Cheddar cheese, grated

60g (2oz) can anchovy fillets
Salt
Pepper

Drain anchovies, and set enough aside to slice to make a thin lattice over the dish. Chop the rest finely.

This page: Macaroni Cheese with Anchovies.

Facing page: Macaroni with Creamy Chicken Sauce (top) and Italian Casserole (bottom).

Italian Casserole

PREPARATION TIME: 15 minutes	
COOKING TIME: 40 minutes	
OVEN: 180°C, 350°F, Gas Mark 4	
SERVES: 4 people	

90g (3oz) small macaroni
60g (2oz) butter or margarine
1 clove garlic, crushed
1 onion, peeled and chopped
2 400g (14oz) cans plum tomatoes
1 tbsp tomato purée
1 red pepper, cored, seeds removed, and chopped roughly
1 green pepper, cored, seeds removed, and chopped roughly
10 black olives, halved, and stones removed
115g (4oz) Mozzarella cheese, sliced thinly
225g (8oz) salami, cut into chunks
Salt
Pepper

Cook the macaroni in plenty of boiling salted water for 10 minutes, or until tender but still firm. Rinse under hot water and drain well. Place in a shallow, oven-proof dish. Meanwhile, heat butter in pan, and fry onion and garlic gently until soft. Add undrained tomatoes, tomato purée, red and green peppers, salami and olives, and stir well. Simmer uncovered for 5 minutes. Season with salt and pepper. Pour over the macaroni, stir, and cover with the sliced cheese. Bake uncovered in a moderate oven for 20 minutes, until cheese has melted. Serve immediately.

Macaroni Cheese with Sausage

PREPARATION TIME: 10 minutes	
COOKING TIME: 20 minutes	
SERVES: 4 people	

225g (8oz) macaroni
60g (2oz) butter or margarine
60g (2oz) flour
600ml (1 pint) milk
1 tsp dry mustard
175g (6oz) Cheddar cheese, grated
8 Frankfurter sausages, or 400g (14oz) can hot-dog sausages
Salt
Pepper

Garnish:
1 pimento, cut into strips

Poach the Frankfurter sausages for 5-8 minutes. Remove skins and, when cold, cut into diagonal slices. (If using hot-dog sausages, just cut as required). Cook macaroni in plenty of boiling salted water for about 10 minutes, or until tender but still firm. Rinse in hot water, and drain well. Meanwhile, melt the butter in a pan. Stir in the flour, and cook for 1 minute. Draw off heat, and gradually add milk, stirring all the time. Bring to the boil, stirring continuously, and cook for 3 minutes. Add sausages, grated cheese, mustard, and salt and pepper to taste. Stir well. Add macaroni, and mix in well. Pour mixture into an oven-proof dish, and sprinkle the remaining cheese over the top. Make a lattice of pimento, and cook under a pre-heated grill until golden brown. Serve immediately.

Pastitsio

PREPARATION TIME: 10 minutes	
COOKING TIME: 1 hour	
OVEN: 190°C, 375°F, Gas Mark 5	
SERVES: 4 people	

225g (8oz) macaroni
90g (3oz) butter or margarine
60g (2oz) Parmesan cheese, grated
Pinch of grated nutmeg
2 eggs, beaten
1 medium onion, peeled and chopped
1 clove garlic, crushed
450g (1lb) minced beef
30ml (2 tbsps) tomato purée
60ml (4 tbsps) red wine
90ml (6 tbsps) beef stock
2 tbsps chopped parsley
30g (1oz) plain flour
300ml (½ pint) milk
Salt
Pepper

Set oven. Cook macaroni in plenty of boiling salted water for 10 minutes, or until tender but still firm. Rinse under hot water. Drain. Put one-third of the butter in the pan and return macaroni to it. Add half the cheese, nutmeg, and salt and pepper to taste. Leave to cool. Mix in half the beaten egg, and put aside. Melt half of the remaining butter in a pan, and fry onion and garlic gently until onion is soft. Increase temperature and add meat, and fry until browned. Add tomato purée, stock, parsley and wine, and season with salt and pepper. Simmer for 20 minutes. In a small pan, melt the rest of the butter. Stir in the flour and cook for 30 seconds. Remove from heat, and stir in milk. Bring to boil, stirring continuously, until the sauce thickens. Beat in the remaining egg and season to taste. Spoon half the macaroni into a serving-dish and cover with the meat sauce. Put on another layer of macaroni and smooth over. Pour over white sauce, and sprinkle with remaining cheese, and bake in the oven for 30 minutes until golden brown. Serve immediately.

Cannelloni with Tomato and Cheese

PREPARATION TIME: 10 minutes	
COOKING TIME: 40 minutes	
OVEN: 210°C, 400°F, Gas Mark 7	
SERVES: 4 people	

12 cannelloni shells

Filling:
400g (14oz) can plum tomatoes
1 tsp tomato purée
1 tsp oregano or basil
115g (4oz) ricotta cheese
115g (4oz) Parmesan cheese, grated
Salt
Pepper

Sauce:
400g (14oz) can plum tomatoes
1 onion, peeled and chopped
15ml (1 tbsp) olive oil
1 tbsp grated Parmesan cheese
1 tbsp cornflour
Salt
Pepper

Cook cannelloni shells in a large pan of boiling salted water for 15-20 minutes until tender. Rinse in hot water and drain well.

Pastitsio (above) and Macaroni Cheese with Sausage (right).

To make filling:

Meanwhile, chop tomatoes and remove pips. Set juice aside for sauce. Beat ricotta cheese until smooth. Add tomato purée, oregano or basil, and Parmesan cheese, and beat well. Finally, stir in chopped tomato and salt and pepper to taste. With a teaspoon, or a piping bag with a wide, plain nozzle, fill the cannelloni shells. Place in an oven-proof dish.

To make sauce:

Heat oil in a saucepan, and cook onion gently until transparent. Push tomatoes and their juice through a sieve into the saucepan. Slake the cornflour with the reserved tomato juice and add to the pan. Bring to the boil and cook for 3 minutes, stirring continuously. Add salt and pepper to taste. Pour over the cannelloni, and sprinkle with cheese. Place in a hot oven, or under a pre-heated grill for 10 minutes or until heated through. Serve immediately.

Spinach Crespelle

PREPARATION TIME: 45 minutes	
COOKING TIME: 30 minutes	
SERVES: 4 people	

12 crespelle:
3 eggs
115g (4oz) plain flour
Pinch of salt
200ml (8 fl oz) water
8ml (½ tbsp) olive oil
30g (1oz) butter or margarine, melted

Filling:
225g (8oz) cream cheese
225g (8oz) packet frozen spinach,
  thawed
30ml (2 tbsps) cream
60g (2oz) Parmesan cheese, grated
½ tsp grated nutmeg
30g (1oz) butter or margarine
Salt
Pepper

To make crespelle:

Sift flour with a pinch of salt. Break eggs into a bowl, and whisk. Add flour gradually, whisking all the time until the mixture is smooth. Add water, and stir in well. Add oil, and mix in. Cover bowl with a damp cloth, and leave in a cool place for 30 minutes. Heat a crêpe pan, or 19cm (7″) frying pan. Grease lightly with melted butter, and put a good tablespoon batter in the centre. Roll the pan to coat

the surface evenly. Fry until crespelle is brown on the underside. Loosen edge with a palette knife, and turn over and brown on the other side. Stack and wrap in a clean cloth until needed.

To make filling:

Cook spinach for 3 minutes in a pan of boiling water. Drain and chop, and set aside. Beat cream cheese and cream together until smooth. Add nutmeg and half the cheese, and salt and pepper to taste, and mix in well. Mix spinach into cream cheese mixture. Divide equally between 12 crespelle, placing mixture at one end, and rolling up. Place in an oven-proof dish, and dot with butter over the top. Sprinkle with Parmesan cheese, and place under a hot grill for 5 minutes, or until browning lightly on top. Serve immediately.

Crespelle with Bolognese Sauce Filling

PREPARATION TIME: 45 minutes	
COOKING TIME: 1 hour 15 minutes	
SERVES: 4 people	

12 crespelle:
3 eggs
115g (4oz) plain flour
Pinch of salt
200ml (8 fl oz) water
8ml (½ tbsp) olive oil
30g (1oz) butter or margarine, melted

Bolognese Sauce:
30g (1oz) butter or margarine
15ml (1 tbsp) olive oil
2 onions, peeled and chopped finely
225g (8oz) minced beef
1 carrot, scraped and chopped finely
115g (4oz) can tomato purée
300ml (½ pint) brown stock
30ml (2 tbsps) sherry
Salt
Pepper

Tomato Sauce:
400g (14oz) can plum tomatoes
½ tsp basil
1 clove garlic, crushed
1 onion, peeled and chopped
15g (½oz) butter
Salt
Pepper

To make Bolognese sauce:

Heat the butter and oil in a pan, and fry the onions and carrot slowly until soft. Increase heat, and add the minced beef. Fry for a few minutes, then stir, cooking until

meat is browned all over. Add the tomato purée, stock, and salt and pepper to taste, and simmer gently for about ¾ hour, until the mixture thickens, stirring occasionally. Add 2 tablespoons sherry, and cook for a further 5 minutes.

To make crespelle:

Sift the flour with a pinch of salt. Break the eggs into a bowl, and whisk. Add the flour gradually, whisking all the time until the mixture is smooth. Add water, and stir in well. Add oil, and mix. Cover bowl with a damp cloth, and leave in a cool place for 30 minutes.

Heat a crêpe pan, or 19cm (7″) frying pan. Grease lightly with the melted butter, and put a good tablespoon of batter in the centre. Roll the pan to coat the surface evenly. Fry until crespelle is brown on the underside. Loosen edge with a palette knife, and turn over and brown the other side. Stack and wrap in a clean cloth until needed.

To make tomato sauce:

Heat butter in pan, and gently fry garlic and basil for 30 seconds. Add onion, and fry until transparent. Add tomatoes, and cook for 10 minutes. Push through a sieve, and return to pan. Add salt and freshly-ground black pepper to taste.

Lay crespelle out, and put 2 heaped tablespoons Bolognese sauce filling at one end of each. Roll up, and place in an oven-proof dish. Repeat until all crespelle have been filled. Put into a hot oven or under a pre-heated grill for 5 minutes. Re-heat tomato sauce, and pour over just before serving. Serve immediately.

Spinach Lasagne

PREPARATION TIME: 10 minutes	
COOKING TIME: 30 minutes	
OVEN: 200°C, 400°F, Gas Mark 7	
SERVES: 4 people	

8 sheets green lasagne pasta

Spinach sauce:
90g (3oz) butter or margarine
325g (11oz) packet of frozen spinach,
  thawed and chopped finely
Pinch of ground nutmeg
90g (3oz) flour
150ml (¼ pint) milk
Salt
Pepper

Mornay sauce:
30g (1oz) butter or margarine
30g (1oz) flour
300ml (½ pint) milk
90g (3oz) Parmesan cheese, grated
1 tsp French mustard
Salt

To make spinach sauce:

Heat butter in pan, stir in flour and cook for 30 seconds. Draw off heat, and stir in milk gradually. Return to heat, and bring to the boil, stirring continuously. Cook for 3 minutes. Add spinach, nutmeg, and salt and pepper to taste. Set aside.

Cook spinach lasagne in lots of boiling salted water for 10 minutes, or until tender. Rinse in cold water, and drain carefully. Dry on a clean cloth.

To make Mornay sauce:

Heat butter in pan and stir in flour, cooking for 30 seconds. Remove from heat, and stir in milk. Return to heat, stirring continuously, until boiling. Continue stirring, and simmer for 3 minutes. Draw off heat, and add mustard and two-thirds of cheese, and salt to taste.

Grease an oven-proof baking dish. Line the base with a layer of lasagne, followed by some of the spinach mixture, and a layer of cheese sauce. Repeat the process, finishing with a layer of lasagne and with a covering of cheese sauce. Sprinkle with the remaining cheese. Bake in a hot oven until golden on top. Serve immediately.

Curried Tuna Cannelloni

PREPARATION TIME: 15 minutes	
COOKING TIME: 45 minutes	
OVEN: 180°C, 350°F, Gas Mark 4	
SERVES: 4 people	

12 cannelloni shells

Filling:
30g (1oz) butter or margarine
1 onion, peeled and chopped
1 stick of celery, chopped

Facing page: Crespelle with Bolognese Sauce Filling (top) and Spinach Crespelle (bottom).

90g (3oz) mushrooms, cleaned and
   chopped
15g (½oz) flour
1 tsp curry powder
150ml (¼ pint) milk
60ml (4 tbsps) soured cream
60ml (4 tbsps) mayonnaise
1 egg, lightly beaten
175g (6oz) can tuna fish
3 shallots, peeled and chopped
Salt
Pepper

Topping:
4 tbsps breadcrumbs
60g (2oz) Cheddar cheese, grated
30g (1oz) butter or margarine

Cook cannelloni shells in a large
pan of boiling salted water for 15-20
minutes until tender. Rinse in hot
water and drain well. Meanwhile,
melt butter in saucepan. Fry onion
until transparent, add mushrooms
and celery, and fry for 5 minutes.
Add curry powder and flour, and
fry until light golden brown. Draw
off the heat, and gradually add milk,
stirring continuously. Return to
heat and bring to the boil. Cook for
3 minutes, stirring all the time. Add
soured cream, mayonnaise, and
undrained flaked tuna. Season with
salt and pepper and stir until sauce
boils. Simmer for 3 minutes. Add

shallots and egg, and mix well.
Spoon mixture into cannelloni
shells, and place in an oven-proof
dish. Sprinkle over a mixture of
breadcrumbs and cheese, and dot
with butter or margarine. Bake in a
moderate oven for 20 minutes.
Serve immediately.

Crab Cannelloni

PREPARATION TIME:	10 minutes
COOKING TIME:	40 minutes
OVEN:	200°C, 400°F, Gas Mark 7
SERVES:	4 people

This page: Spinach Lasagne.

**Facing page: Curried Tuna
Cannelloni (top) and Crab
Cannelloni (bottom).**

12 cannelloni shells

Filling:
225g (8oz) fresh crab meat (or frozen
   crab meat, thawed)
30g (1oz) butter or margarine
3 shallots, peeled and chopped

½ tsp Worcestershire sauce
1 tsp French mustard
Salt
Pepper

Mornay sauce:

30g (1oz) butter or margarine
30g (1oz) flour
300ml (½ pint) milk
60g (2oz) Cheddar or Parmesan
    cheese, grated
Salt
Pepper

Cook cannelloni shells in a large pan of boiling salted water for 15-20 minutes until tender. Rinse in hot water and drain well. Meanwhile, heat butter in pan. Add shallots, crab meat, Worcestershire sauce, mustard, salt and pepper, and stir until heated through. Fill cannelloni shells with crab mixture, using a piping bag with a wide, plain nozzle, or a teaspoon. Place in an oven-proof dish.

To make Mornay sauce:

Heat butter in pan, and stir in flour. Remove from heat and gradually add milk. Return to heat, and bring to boil. Cook for 3 minutes, stirring continuously. Stir in half the cheese until it melts. Do not reboil. Season with salt and pepper. Pour over the cannelloni and sprinkle with remaining cheese. Place in a hot oven, or under a pre-heated grill until golden brown. Serve immediately.

Lasagne Rolls

PREPARATION TIME: 5 minutes	
COOKING TIME: 15 minutes	
SERVES: 4 people	

8 sheets of lasagne pasta
225g (8oz) chicken breast fillets
60g (2oz) butter or margarine
60g (2oz) Gruyère or Cheddar
    cheese, grated
30g (1oz) flour
150ml (¼ pint) milk
60g (2oz) button mushrooms
2 tsps oil
Salt
Pepper

In a large saucepan, fill two-thirds with boiling salted water and 2 teaspoons oil. Bring to the boil. Add 1 sheet of lasagne; wait about 2 minutes, and add another sheet. Only cook a few at a time. When tender, remove, and rinse under cold water, and leave to drain. Repeat until all the lasagne is cooked. Meanwhile, wash and slice mushrooms, and slice chicken. Put half the butter in a small frying pan, and fry the mushrooms and chicken. In a small saucepan, melt the rest of the butter. Add the flour, and cook for a minute. Remove from the heat, and add the milk. Mix well and bring to the boil. Cook for 3 minutes. Add sauce to chicken and mushrooms, and add half the cheese, mixing well. Add salt and pepper to taste. Spread out lasagne, and spread one-eighth mixture at one end of each. Roll up each piece of lasagne, and put into an oven-proof dish. Sprinkle with remaining cheese, and put under a pre-heated grill until golden brown. Serve immediately.

Lasagne

PREPARATION TIME: 10 minutes	
COOKING TIME: 45 minutes	
OVEN: 200°C, 400°F, Gas Mark 7	
SERVES: 4 people	

8 sheets of lasagne pasta

Meat sauce:

90g (3oz) butter or margarine
1 carrot, diced
1 celery stick, diced
1 onion, peeled and diced
90g (3oz) minced beef
1 tsp marjoram
1 tbsp flour
1 tbsp tomato purée
150ml (¼ pint) beef stock
Salt
Pepper

Béchamel sauce:

60g (2oz) butter or margarine
45g (1½oz) flour
300ml (½ pint) milk
6 peppercorns
1 bay leaf
Slice of onion
Parsley stalks

To make meat sauce:

Heat butter in pan and add onion, celery and carrot. Cook until golden. Add minced beef, and brown well. Stir in flour; add tomato purée, beef stock, marjoram, and salt and pepper. Cook for 15 minutes.

Meanwhile, cook the lasagne in lots of boiling salted water for 10 minutes, or until tender. Rinse in cold water and drain carefully. Lay out on a clean cloth to dry.

To make Béchamel sauce:

Heat milk in a saucepan with peppercorns, slice of onion, bay leaf and parsley stalks. Bring to simmering point and remove from heat. Allow to cool for 5 minutes. Strain. Melt butter in a saucepan. Stir in flour and cook for 30 seconds. Remove from heat and gradually add milk, stirring continuously. Cook for 3 minutes.

Grease an oven-proof baking dish. Line base with a layer of lasagne sheets. Cover with a layer of meat sauce, and a layer of Bechamel sauce. Place another layer of lasagne, repeating until all the ingredients are used, finishing with a layer of lasagne and a layer of Béchamel sauce. Bake in a hot oven until the top is golden. Serve immediately.

Lasagne Rolls (above right) and Lasagne (below right).

Desserts

Vanilla Cream Melba

PREPARATION TIME: 15 minutes

COOKING TIME: 10 minutes

SERVES: 4 people

90g (3oz) soup pasta
450ml (¾ pint) milk
45g (1½oz) brown sugar
150ml (¼ pint) cream, lightly
    whipped
Few drops vanilla essence
1 can peach halves
1 tsp cinnamon

Melba sauce:
225g (8oz) raspberries
30g (1oz) icing sugar

Cook pasta in milk and sugar until soft. Stir regularly, being careful not to allow it to boil over. Draw off heat and stir in vanilla essence. Pour pasta into a bowl to cool. When cool, fold in cream. Chill. Meanwhile, make Melba sauce. Push raspberries through a sieve. Mix in icing sugar to desired thickness and taste. Serve pasta with peach halves and Melba sauce. Dust with cinnamon if desired.

Black Cherry Ravioli with Soured Cream Sauce

PREPARATION TIME: 30 minutes

COOKING TIME: 15 minutes

SERVES: 4 people

Dough:
275g (9oz) strong plain flour
1 tbsp sugar
3 eggs

Large can black cherries, pips
    removed
60g (2oz) granulated sugar
1 tsp arrowroot
115ml (4 fl oz) soured cream
115ml (4 fl oz) double cream

Put cherries in a sieve. Strain off juice and reserve. Make dough by sifting flour and sugar in a bowl. Make a well in the centre and add lightly-beaten eggs. Work flour and eggs together with a spoon, and then by hand, until a smooth dough is formed. Knead gently. Lightly flour board, and roll dough out thinly into a rectangle. Cut dough in half. Put well-drained cherries about 4cm (1½") apart on the dough. Place the other half on top, and cut with a small glass or pastry cutter. Seal well around edges with the back of a fork. Boil plenty of water in a large saucepan, and drop in cherry pasta. Cook for about 10 minutes, or until they rise to the surface. Remove with a draining spoon and keep warm.

This page: Black Cherry Ravioli with Soured Cream Sauce.

Facing page: Vanilla Cream Melba (top) and Chocolate Cream Helène (bottom).

Keep 2 tablespoons cherry juice aside. Mix 1 tablespoon cherry juice with arrowroot; mix remaining juice with sugar and set over heat. Add arrowroot mixture, and heat until it thickens. Meanwhile mix soured cream and double cream together, and marble 1 tablespoon of cherry juice through it. Pour hot, thickened cherry juice over cherry ravioli. Serve hot with cream sauce.

Chocolate Cream Helène

PREPARATION TIME: 15 minutes	
COOKING TIME: 10 minutes	
SERVES: 4 people	

90g (3oz) soup pasta
450ml (¾ pint) milk
45g (1½oz) caster sugar
150ml (¼ pint) cream, lightly
   whipped
1 tsp cocoa
1 tbsp hot water
1 large can pear halves

Garnish:
Chocolate, grated

Cook pasta in milk and sugar until soft. Stir regularly, being careful not to allow it to boil over. Meanwhile, dissolve cocoa in hot water, and stir into pasta. Pour pasta into a bowl to cool. When cool, fold in lightly-whipped cream. Chill. Serve with pear halves, and a sprinkling of grated chocolate.

Honey Vermicelli

PREPARATION TIME: 1 hour	
COOKING TIME: 15 minutes	
SERVES: 4 people	

225g (8oz) vermicelli
60g (2oz) butter
3 tbsps clear honey
2 tsps sesame seeds
¼ tsp cinnamon

Sauce:
75ml (5 tbsps) double cream
75ml (5 tbsps) soured cream

Cook vermicelli in boiling salted water for 5 minutes or until tender, stirring regularly with a fork to separate noodles. Drain, and spread out to dry on a wire tray covered with absorbent paper or a tea-towel. Leave for about an hour. Make sauce by mixing soured cream and double cream together. Melt butter in frying pan. Add sesame seeds, and fry until lightly golden. Stir in honey, cinnamon and vermicelli, and heat through. Serve hot, topped with cream sauce.

Cream Cheese Margherita

PREPARATION TIME: 1 hour	
COOKING TIME: 10 minutes	
SERVES: 4 people	

115g (4oz) soup pasta
150ml (¼ pint) single cream
225g (8oz) packet cream cheese
½ tsp ground cinnamon
60g (2oz) caster sugar
60g (2oz) sultanas
Juice and grated rind of ½ a lemon

Garnish:
1 tbsp flaked almonds
Lemon peel, cut into slivers

Soak sultanas in lemon juice for about 1 hour. Meanwhile, cook the pasta in plenty of boiling, lightly-salted water until tender, stirring occasionally. Work the cream cheese, sugar and cream together until smooth. Beat in grated lemon rind and cinnamon. Fold in pasta and sultanas. Divide between individual dessert glasses or small sweet dishes, and cover top with flaked almond and slivers of lemon peel. Chill.

Honey Vermicelli (top right) and Cream Cheese Margherita (right).

Index